Core Teachings of
the Dalai Lama

Perfecting Patience

*Buddhist Techniques to
Overcome Anger*

The Dalai Lama

TRANSLATED BY
Thupten Jinpa

SNOW LION
BOULDER
2018

Shambhala Publications, Inc.
4720 Walnut Street
Boulder, Colorado 80301
www.shambhala.com

Quotations of Shantideva's *Guide to the Bodhisattva's Way of Life* are
from Stephen Batchelor's translation, published by the Library of Tibetan
Works and Archives, Dharamsala, India, in 1979.

This book was previously published under the title *Healing Anger*.

9 8 7 6 5 4 3 2 1

Printed in the United States of America

∞ This edition is printed on acid-free paper that meets the American
National Standards Institute z39.48 Standard.
♻ This book is printed on 30% recycled paper. For more information
please visit www.shambhala.com.

Shambhala Publications is distributed worldwide by Penguin Random
House, Inc., and its subsidiaries.

Library of Congress Cataloging-in-Publication Data
Names: Bstan-'dzin-rgya-mtsho, Dalai Lama XIV, 1935– author. | Thupten
Jinpa, translator. | Śāntideva, active 7th century. Bodhicaryāvatāra.
Title: Perfecting patience: Buddhist techniques to overcome anger/
The Dalai Lama; translated by Thupten Jinpa. Other titles: Healing
anger | Description: Boulder, Colorado Shambhala, 2018. | Series: Core
teachings of the Dalai Lama series | "Quotations of Shantideva's Guide to
the Bodhisattva's Way of Life are from Stephen Batchelor's translation,
published by the Library of Tibetan Works and Archives, Dharamsala,
India, in 1979. This book was previously published under the title Healing
Anger." | Includes bibliographical references and index.
Identifiers: LCCN 2018012744 | ISBN 9781559394796 (paperback)
Subjects: LCSH: Śāntideva, active 7th century. Bodhicaryāvatāra. |
Patience—Religious aspects—Buddhism. | Buddhism--Doctrines. | BISAC:
RELIGION/Buddhism/Tibetan. | RELIGION / Buddhism / Rituals &
Practice. Classification: LCC BQ3147.B775 2018 | DDC 294.3/5—dc23
LC record available at https://lccn.loc.gov/2018012744

CONTENTS

FOREWORD

A LL BUDDHIST TEACHINGS begin with a teacher and a student, and the 1993 teachings by His Holiness the Dalai Lama in Phoenix and Tucson, Arizona, were no exception.

As early as 1986, Howard C. Cutler, MD, requested that His Holiness come to Arizona. His invitation was accepted in 1990, and in September of that year he invited Lopön Claude d'Estrée to join him in requesting specific dates. Finally, in the summer of 1992, word came that His Holiness had agreed to teach in Arizona in the fall of 1993. His Holiness asked what he should teach, and Howard and Claude replied that he should teach whatever he would like to teach. His Holiness then stated that it was the responsibility of the host to determine what would best serve the needs of the students.

It didn't take long for Howard to suggest Shantideva's teaching on patience. Why patience? First, we wanted to request a teaching that would be universal in scope, one that would appeal to Buddhists and non-Buddhists alike. Second, we wanted to request a topic that would be very practical, that one could bring into everyday life. Third, we felt that a lack of understanding of patience, and its reflection in the overwhelming dominance of anger, was endemic to our culture. Anger is one of the roots that cause so much unhappiness, suffering, discord, and violence in our world. It is expressed hundreds of times a day in the mass media, especially television. It is found in how we settle disputes in our highly litigious society; in how our leaders conduct themselves in the halls of Congress; in the increase of domestic violence and child abuse; and in the sense of self-hating and self-loathing that pervades our culture. Politeness, kindness, patience, and compassion often seem a part of our mythical past.

Shantideva states in the very beginning of his chapter on patience that one moment of anger can wipe out a lifetime of merit. At first this seems a harsh statement, but upon reflection it makes a great deal of sense. When we get angry with someone we are often unaware of the effect it has on that person, let alone the ripple effect it causes. Nonetheless, it does indeed have a ripple effect: that person does not hang on to the anger but passes it on, perhaps repeatedly. The antidote to anger is patience, and so the dissemination of Shantideva's wisdom regarding patience becomes a critical need in these times.

In the course of developing this series of teachings, Arizona Teachings, Inc. was formed with Dr. Cutler, Lopön d'Estrée, and Ken Bacher as founding directors. We decided to take a new approach to the presentation of a teaching by His Holiness. In the past, His Holiness would stay at a nice hotel, a large hall would be rented, and the students would stay at a variety of hotels and motels in the area. Our vision was to have a place where His Holiness could stay that could also accommodate both the teaching hall and the students. In essence we wanted to create a "campus" for five days where everyone who attended the teachings could relax and enjoy each other's company. It was important that the setting be beautiful and peaceful, a place where His Holiness and his entourage, lay students, and their families would feel enriched by the natural setting. We chose the Sheraton El Conquistador Resort, surrounded by the Sonora Desert with a backdrop of the Catalina Mountains in Oro Valley just north of Tucson.

The morning of His Holiness' arrival in Tucson was marked by deep blue desert skies and a double rainbow as we approached Oro Valley. On seeing the natural beauty of the setting for the teachings, His Holiness exclaimed that it reminded him very much of Lhasa.

And so, with these good omens, on September 11, 1993, in the Year of the Water Bird, at Pusch Ridge in the state of Arizona, numberless gods and demigods, 1,600 humans and bodhisattvas, asuras, and gandharvas assembled to hear His Holiness Tenzin Gyatso, the Fourteenth Dalai Lama of Tibet and the living incarnation of Bodhisattva Avalokiteshvara, present and comment on Acharya Shantideva's teaching on patience and the bodhisattva's way of life. We pray that these teachings are of benefit to all sentient beings.

ACKNOWLEDGMENTS

Funding and support of Arizona Friends of Tibet, and particularly its president, Peggy Hitchcock, made it possible for our fledgling organization to announce the teachings and begin the myriad arrangements required for the visit. Most of the details of the visit were handled by nearly three dozen volunteers, coordinated by Bonnie Cheney. Computer record-keeping systems were created by Dan Crowell, G. Greg Bender, and Richard Laue.

Volunteers transcribed the teachings presented in this book from the sixteen hours of oral teachings delivered by His Holiness: thanks go particularly to Julie Jones, Karen Garland, Amy Zehra Conner, and Julie Montgomery. The transcript was then edited by Ken Bacher and put into final form by Kate Bloodgood and Susan Kyser of Snow Lion Publications, with crucial assistance from Geshe Thupten Jinpa. Some small liberties have been taken with the arrangement of the transcribed material to more effectively present it in book form; the editors, however, have striven to preserve the voice of the Dalai Lama as much as possible.

None of this would have been possible without the cooperation and support of Kazur Tenzin Geyche Tethong, His Holiness' private secretary, and his staff; Rinchen Dharlo of the Office of Tibet in New York; and Geshe Thupten Jinpa, who served as His Holiness' interpreter during the teachings.

Finally, our very special thanks go to His Holiness, Tenzin Gyatso, the Fourteenth Dalai Lama of Tibet, our teacher and example, for his kindness in offering these teachings to all of us in Arizona and to the world at large. His Holiness' personal practice of patience is an inspiration to us all. May he live long to turn the Wheel of Dharma for his people and for all people around the world who look to him as an example of enlightened compassion and kindness in a world too filled with distrust, conflict, and anger.

May all sentient beings benefit.

Lopön Claude d'Estrée
Ken Bacher
Arizona Teachings, Inc.

Publisher's Acknowledgment

Snow Lion Publications gratefully acknowledges the generous support of the Gere Foundation and Tibet Fund in sponsoring the production of this book.

THE CHALLENGE OF PATIENCE
Translator's Introduction

A POPULAR STORY THAT Tibetan teachers are fond of telling their students narrates an encounter between a hermit and a herdsman:

> The hermit was living alone in the mountains. One day, a herdsman happened to pass by his cave. Intrigued, the herdsman shouted at the hermit and asked, "What are you doing alone in the middle of nowhere?"
>
> The hermit replied, "I am meditating."
>
> "What are you meditating on?" asked the herdsman.
>
> "On patience," said the hermit.
>
> There was a moment of silence. After a while, the herdsman decided to leave. Just as he turned to go, he looked back at the hermit and shouted, "By the way, you go to hell!"
>
> "What do you mean? *You* go to hell!" came flying back.
>
> The herdsman laughed and reminded the hermit that he was supposed to be practicing patience!

This simple story wonderfully illustrates the key challenge for someone who wishes to practice patience: in a situation which would ordinarily give rise to an outburst of anger, how can we maintain spontaneity and yet remain calm in our response? This challenge is not restricted to religious practitioners alone. It is a challenge each of us faces as we try to live our lives with a degree of human dignity and decency. At nearly every turn we are confronted with situations that test the limits of our patience and tolerance. Be it within our family, in the work environment, or simply when interacting with others, often our prejudices are revealed, our beliefs challenged, and our self-image threatened. It is in these moments that our inner resources are most called upon. All of this, Shantideva would say, tests our character, revealing how far we have developed our capacity for patience and tolerance.

The story also tells us that patience is something that cannot be cultivated in isolation from other people. In fact, it is a quality that can arise only within the context of our interaction with others, especially with fellow human beings. The hermit's spontaneous response shows his inner development to have been as unstable as a child's sandcastle. It is one thing to immerse oneself in warm thoughts of tolerance and compassion toward others in the unchallenged environment of solitude, but it is entirely a different matter to live these ideals in one's day-to-day interactions with real people. This is of course not to belittle the importance of silent meditation. Such solitary practices internalize insights which otherwise would remain only at the level of intellectual knowledge. And, like most ancient Indian religious traditions, Buddhism advocates meditation as a key element of the spiritual path. But the fact remains that the true test of patience comes only in the context of interaction with others.

The third point that we can observe in the brief encounter between our hermit and the herdsman is that genuine patience is developed only when one has gained some degree of control over one's anger. Of course, reacting with an outburst of strong emotion at unprovoked verbal abuse is a natural human response. But a genuine spiritual person should be capable of going beyond such predictable human responses. This is what Shantideva teaches us in the "Patience" chapter of his *Guide to the Bodhisattva's Way of Life*. And in His Holiness the Dalai Lama's lucid commentary, we have a clear exposition of the ideals and practices aimed at cultivating and perfecting the vital spiritual quality of patience.

The teachings on patience presented in this volume are essential components of what is known in Mahayana Buddhism as the Bodhisattva ideal, namely the selfless ideals of the spiritual aspirant who dedicates his or her entire life toward others' welfare. Does the Bodhisattva ideal elevate meekness and submission to high, spiritual principles? Does it advocate tolerance toward evil? What about justified anger and hatred? Isn't what the Bodhisattva ideal asks of us impossible because it goes against basic human nature? These are some of the questions that immediately come to mind for modern readers of Shantideva.

SHANTIDEVA AND HIS *GUIDE TO THE BODHISATTVA'S WAY OF LIFE*

Before we proceed further in our discussion of patience, a few words on Shantideva's *Guide to the Bodhisattva's Way of Life,* the sixth chapter of which forms the core of the Dalai Lama's teachings in this book, are in order. Written in the eighth century C.E., Shantideva's work soon became an important classic of Mahayana Buddhism. Legend has it that Shantideva recited the entire text extemporaneously when he was asked to give a lecture to a congregation of monks at the famous Indian monastic university of Nalanda. It is said that the request to teach initially arose out of a desire to humiliate Shantideva, whom his fellow monks saw as doing nothing but "eating, sleeping, and defecating." Little did the monks realize that while Shantideva appeared to be leading a somewhat lazy life, he was in fact rich in inner experience and profound learning. Tibetan accounts of the story maintain that when Shantideva reached the difficult ninth chapter, the chapter on wisdom, he started to ascend into the air and began to disappear although his voice could still be heard.

Whatever the merits of this legend, the importance of the *Guide to the Bodhisattva's Way of Life* in the cultural and temporal milieu of Indian literature cannot be underestimated. Shantideva's text became one of the most celebrated Buddhist works. For the religious practitioner it became an important scripture outlining the essential practices of the Mahayana Buddhist path to enlightenment. Of all the religious writings of the Mahayana Buddhist tradition, it could be said that Shantideva's *Guide* and Nagarjuna's *Precious Garland* together remain the foundational texts outlining the noble, selfless career of the Bodhisattva. For scholars and philosophers, the ninth chapter represents an important contribution to the development of the Buddhist philosophy of the "middle way." And for ordinary Buddhists, the text became a profound source of inspiration in their own personal faith. To this day, the chapter of dedication, the tenth and last chapter, remains one of the most passionate expressions of profound religious sentiment in Mahayana Buddhist literature.

The impact of Shantideva's *Guide* in Tibet was perhaps unsurpassed. Ever since its translation into Tibetan in the eleventh century, the work exerted a powerful influence upon the religious life of the Tibetan people. Its pervasive influence can be found in the teachings of all four major schools of Tibetan Buddhism: Nyingma, Sakya, Kagyu, and Gelug. In addition to giving rise to extensive scholarship related to the Mahayana ideals and practices that are treated extensively in the work, the text also led to the development of a whole new genre of literature which became collectively known as *lo-jong* or "the training of mind." This is a category of religious writings which deal primarily with two central concerns of Shantideva's work, namely the cultivation of the altruistic mind of awakening and the generation of profound insight into the nature of reality. As evidence of the text's great inspirational power, those who have attended any talks by the Dalai Lama will recall the liberty with which he quotes from Shantideva's *Guide*. The following stanza is now almost immortalized because of the Dalai Lama's repeated statements that it is his greatest source of inspiration:

> For as long as space endures
> And for as long as living beings remain,

Until then may I too abide
To dispel the misery in the world. *(Guide,* X:55)

It became customary in Tibet for aspiring young novices to memorize the entire text of Shantideva's *Guide* so that the stanzas could be sung in group recitations. In its Tibetan translation, the work exists entirely in verse, each stanza containing four perfectly metered lines. To this day, I remember with joy the nights I spent in group recitations marvelling at the poetic beauty and the profundity of Shantideva's verses at Ganden Monastery in South India where I received my own monastic education.

Earlier we entertained some of the questions which might be posed by the modern reader of Shantideva. I shall allow Shantideva's own verses and the Dalai Lama's clear commentary to speak for themselves. However, as the translator of the Dalai Lama's teachings I shall endeavor to provide some words of explanation which may help to present a useful background to both Shantideva and the Dalai Lama's insights. In doing so, I also hope to help situate the teachings contained in this volume in a wider context.

The Tibetan word *soe-pa,* which is here translated as "patience," has various connotations. Literally speaking, *soe-pa* means "forbearance," and in its verbal form it means "to withstand" or "to endure something," as in the case of "to endure hardships." However, when *soe-pa* is used to describe a quality, as in the case of a person's character, its meaning is best understood as "tolerance." In Tibetan, a person who possesses a developed character of tolerance is said to be "great in *soe-pa.*" Yet "tolerance" alone does not capture the complete meaning of *soe-pa,* for it is possible for someone to have a tolerant temperament yet be quite impatient. In contrast, a person who is "great in *soe-pa*" is said to have a patient temperament too. Of course, I am not suggesting that the Tibetan term should be translated as "patience/tolerance/forbearance," for doing so would go against all established canons of writing. What I do wish to do here is draw attention to the multifaceted meaning of the Tibetan term so that the reader is at least aware of the complexity of the concepts involved.

By advocating the practice of patience, Shantideva is not suggesting that we should simply submit ourselves to abuse and exploitation from others. Nor is he recommending a policy of simple, unquestioned acceptance of suffering and pain. What he is advocating is a resolute stand against adversities. In his commentary, the Dalai Lama draws a distinction between meekness and tolerance. He suggests that genuine tolerance can only arise where one has consciously adopted a stance not to retaliate against an actual or perceived harm. The crucial point here is the "consciously adopted stand." Although neither Shantideva nor the Dalai Lama gives an explicit definition of patience, we can take the following as a working definition. "Patience" (*soe-pa*), according to the Buddhist understanding of the principle, is "a resolute response against adversity stemming from a settled temperament unperturbed by either external or internal disturbance." Certainly, this cannot be described as a passive submission; rather it is an active approach toward adversity. Shantideva's discussion of patience takes place within the framework of what could be called the three characteristics of patience. They are: (1) tolerance based on conscious acceptance of pain and hardships, (2) tolerance resulting from reflecting on the nature of reality, and (3) tolerance toward injuries from others.

Shantideva discusses the first aspect of patience in verses 12 through 21. He begins by observing that pain and suffering are natural facts of existence and that denying this truth can only cause additional misery. He then goes on to argue that if we could internalize this fundamental truth of our existence, we would derive enormous benefit in our day-to-day life. For one thing, we would see suffering as a catalyst for spiritual growth. Shantideva implies that a person who is capable of responding to suffering in this way can voluntarily accept the pain and hardship involved in seeking to achieve a higher purpose. In theory, we are all aware of this principle. To protect ourselves against tropical diseases we often submit willingly to the pain of inoculations. In arguing that it is possible to train ourselves to accept greater pain than we are capable of now, Shantideva writes the following memorable lines:

> There is nothing whatsoever
> That is not made easier through acquaintance.
> So through becoming acquainted with small harms
> I should learn to patiently accept greater harms.
> (*Guide*, VI:14)

He concludes the discussion of the first characteristic of patience by drawing attention to the positive aspects of suffering, if anything at all can be described as "positive" about pain and suffering. Shantideva asserts that it is our experience of suffering that awakens us from our spiritual slumbers. It is also suffering that enables us to identify with others' pain, thus allowing us to generate genuine compassion for them. Furthermore, it is suffering that instills within us the fear of evil so crucial for the religious person. Finally, it is our insight into suffering that reinforces our longing for spiritual freedom. Of course, many of these sentiments can be said to be religious, which a modern reader may perhaps argue as being relevant only to a religious practitioner. But the basic insight of Shantideva stands. That is to say that if approached with the appropriate attitude, even pain and suffering can be perceived in terms of their positive effects.

Verses 22 through 34 discuss the second aspect of patience: tolerance based on understanding the nature of reality. The main focus of Shantideva's argument here is demonstrating how actions of people and events are determined by a network of many factors. This is to underline the critical fact that many of the conditions which cause others to act in ways that are harmful to us are in fact outside their control. As Shantideva puts it, we become ill without wishing to be so. Similarly, we do not intend to be angry, but often find ourselves gripped with anger. So one could argue that in a sense it is illogical to isolate from the complex conditions only the person and hold him or her alone responsible for the act of harm. To illustrate this argument, Shantideva presents an unusual analysis of the simple act of someone hitting us with a stick. He shows how both the stick and the person who wields it are equally responsible for causing the pain. On a deeper level, he argues, even the mere fact that we possess corporeal existence is an important contributory factor in generating the pain. A further condition, which in fact turns out to be the key cause, is the negative emotion which motivated the person to inflict the harm in the first place.

It is obvious that the principle underlying the second aspect of patience is nothing but the fundamental Buddhist principle of dependent origination. In this view, nothing arises in isolation, for everything comes into being due to the aggregation of multiple causes and conditions. Since this principle can be understood at many levels—in terms of causal dependence, in terms of mutuality of concepts, or in terms of interdependence between our perceptions and the world—the insights into reality which give rise to greater tolerance toward events and others' actions can also vary in their depth. For example, Shantideva demonstrates how viewing the world as illusion-like can have immediate impact in reducing the intensity of our strong emotional reactions like anger. Shantideva writes the following to make this point:

> Hence everything is governed by other factors (which in
>   turn) are governed by (others),
> And in this way nothing governs itself.
> Having understood this, I should not become angry
> With phenomena that are like apparitions. (*Guide,* VI:31)

These lines echo similar observations Shantideva makes in the ninth chapter of his *Guide.* There, after arguing for the Buddhist philosophical world view based on an appreciation of the nonsubstantial nature of phenomena, Shantideva poses the following rhetorical questions: What is there to obtain or lose? Who is there to praise or insult? Whence do joy and pain arise? What is there to be happy or sad about? On the surface, it may seem that Shantideva is advocating a form of apathetic equanimity. But to read his verses in this way is to totally miss the point. Like all skillful teachers of Buddhism, Shantideva is drawing our attention to the intimate link between attachment and strong emotions like anger. The more we are attached to something, the more likely it is to make us angry when we perceive a threat to that object of attachment. Although Shantideva's discussion of tolerance based on insight into the nature of reality is situated within the Buddhist philosophical discourse, I think his basic argument does not depend upon the validity of Buddhist theories about reality. From our own experience, we can see that the deeper our appreciation of the complexity of the circumstances giving rise to an event, the greater our ability to respond to that event with a degree of calmness and tolerance.

We have now come to the final characteristic of patience: tolerance toward injuries from others. Perhaps it is because of its overwhelming importance that Shantideva treats this category last (in verses 34 through 63). One could say that of the three dimensions of patience the third is probably the most important, because it exclusively pertains to our immediate interaction with others. There is no denying that for most of us the main object of our anger or frustration is often a fellow human. And, until we learn to interact with others in a way that is not tainted by strong negative emotions such as anger, no genuine development of patience can take place. This is especially true for a practitioner of the Bodhisattva ideal whose avowed aim is to help liberate all beings from a state of unenlightened existence. Of course, to such a person, being angry toward the very object for whose salvation he or she has taken a solemn religious pledge is most inappropriate.

Shantideva teaches us that it is more appropriate to have compassion rather than anger toward those who cause harm to us. He suggests that those who cause harm to others are in some sense possessed. In other words, their actions stem from a state of ignorance. This is reminiscent of the Christian Gospel's injunction that we must forgive the perpetrators of evil, "for they know not what they do." In fact, Shantideva asks us to go further and regard those who harm us, our enemies, as precious, for they alone give us the rare opportunity to practice tolerance. He writes:

> There are indeed many beggars in this world,
> But scarce are those that inflict harm;
> For if I have not injured others
> Few beings will cause me harm.

> Therefore, just like treasure appearing in my house
> Without any effort on my part to obtain it,
> I should be happy to have an enemy
> For he assists me in my conduct of Awakening. (*Guide,* VI:
> 106–107)

It is verses like this which provide the basis for the Dalai Lama's often quoted statement that our enemy is our greatest teacher. He has certainly applied these principles in his dealing with the Chinese authorities who have caused so much harm and destruction to his people and homeland. Once we understand that his thought is rooted in such spiritual training, we will have no difficulty accepting the Dalai Lama's claim that he and his people bear no hatred toward the Chinese.

At times, Shantideva presents arguments which appear to take rationalization to the extreme. For example, there is an intriguing argument to illustrate the futility of anger as a response to others' harmful actions. Shantideva suggests that we examine whether inflicting harm on others is essential to human nature or if it is an accidental quality. If it is the former, Shantideva argues, it is pointless to be angry, for this would be like begrudging fire because of its inherent capacity to burn. On the other hand, he argues, if it is an accidental quality it is still inappropriate to respond with anger, since this would be like begrudging the sky for being overcast! Either way, he concludes, there are no logical grounds for being angry. Regardless of its merits as an argument, no one can dispute its ingenuity. The question is: how seriously should we take this kind of argument? Certainly, there is no denying that from a general reader's point of view these forms of argument can at best be appreciated as "thought experiments." We know that often we tend to reinforce our anger or outrage when we strongly feel that we are in the right. If this is true, then even a modern reader of Shantideva can accept the value of this kind of thought experiment, which poignantly reveals the illogical nature of having strong emotional reactions to an event.

ON DEALING WITH ANGER

Undoubtedly, both Shantideva and the Dalai Lama are most articulate in their discourse on how to deal with anger and hatred. Shantideva in fact opens the chapter on patience with the strong statement that an instance of anger can destroy positive imprints created over "a thousand eons." He further asserts that there is no evil like hatred and that there is no fortitude like patience. Thus, he recommends that we all seek to develop patience. In Shantideva's view, anger acts as the principal obstacle to the development of patience. To use the well-known medical analogy, hatred is the poison and patience is the medicine that removes the poisonous toxins from within the mind. As the Dalai Lama's commentary makes clear, Shantideva identifies two key elements in our attempts to overcome anger. First and foremost, it is important for us to have a profound appreciation of the negativity of anger. Of particular relevance is to reflect upon the destructive effects of generating anger. Second, Shantideva identifies the need to develop a deep understanding of the causal mechanism which underlies the arisal of anger. This is of special interest to the modern reader, who will unavoidably be approaching Shantideva's text with many of the popular assumptions associated with modern psychology and its views on human emotions.

In verse 7 of the chapter, Shantideva makes the crucial observation that the "fuel" of anger is what he calls "mental discomfort."

This is an interesting notion. The Tibetan word is *yi mi-dewa* which can be translated as "dejection," "unhappiness," or simply as "dissatisfaction." It is best understood as a pervasive, underlying sense of dissatisfaction, which need not be felt at the conscious level. It is that nagging feeling that something is not quite right. Shantideva seems to be suggesting that it is this underlying sense of dissatisfaction that gives rise to frustration. When this happens, the conditions are set for an immediate outburst of anger when things do not go the way we wish. Once this causal nexus between dissatisfaction, frustration, and anger is understood, we can then appreciate the virtue of Shantideva's approach to dealing with anger. We can see that much of his approach is aimed at rooting out this underlying sense of dissatisfaction rather than engaging in a head-to-head confrontation with actual full-blown anger. This is the reason for Shantideva's emphasis on reflections which aim to create stability of mind. As to the specific practices, the reader can follow the detailed commentary of the Dalai Lama in the appropriate sections of the book.

An important point to note here is that Shantideva does not appear to make any distinction between anger and hatred in his discussion. However, the Dalai Lama's commentary explicitly underlines this critical distinction. He observes that, in principle, it may be possible to accept what could be called a "positive anger." Anger as an outrage toward injustice done to others can often be an important catalyst for powerful altruistic deeds. However, he rejects such possibility with regard to hatred. For the Dalai Lama, hatred can have no virtue. It only eats the person from within and poisons his or her interactions with fellow human beings. In his words, "Hatred is the true enemy; it is the inner enemy." Perhaps we can say that the feature that distinguishes anger and hatred is the absence or presence of ill-will. A person can be angry without bearing any ill-will toward his or her object of anger. The Dalai Lama instructs us to ensure that our anger, even when it arises, never culminates in full-blown hatred. This, I think, is an important ethical teaching.

A few words on some of the general principles which lie behind the approaches suggested in this book for dealing with our emotions and developing patience may perhaps help the general reader. A key principle is a belief in what could be called the plasticity of the mind, that is, an assumption of the mind's limitless capacity for improvement. This is supported by a complex understanding of the psychology of the mind and its various modalities. Both Shantideva and the Dalai Lama are operating within a long history of Buddhist psychology and philosophy of mind which emphasizes a detailed analysis of human emotions. Generally speaking, in this view the mind is perceived in terms of a complex, dynamic system where both cognitive and affective dimensions of the psyche are seen as an integrated whole. So, when the two masters present means of dealing with emotions such as anger, they are not suggesting that we should suppress them. Both Buddhist and modern psychology agree on the harmfulness of mere suppression. The Buddhist approach is to get at the root so that the very basis for anger is undercut. In other words, Shantideva and the Dalai Lama are suggesting ways of reorienting our character so that we become less prone to strong reactive emotions such as anger. It is in this light that most of the reflections recommended in this volume should be understood. The motto is simple: Discipline your mind. Shantideva underlines the critical importance of this inner discipline with a wonderful analogy:

> Where would I possibly find enough leather
> With which to cover the surface of the earth?
> But (wearing) just leather on the soles of my shoes
> Is equivalent to covering the earth with it.
> Likewise it is not possible for me
> To restrain the external course of things;
> But should I restrain this mind of mine
> What would be the need to restrain all else?
> (*Guide*, V:13–14)

This of course is reminiscent of the memorable verse from the *Dhammapada* in which the Buddha says:

> Intangible and subtle is the mind,
> That flies after fancies as it likes;
> Wise are those who discipline their minds,
> For a mind well-disciplined brings great joy. (Verse 35)

Shantideva calls this basic Buddhist practice "guarding the mind" and he discusses it at great length in chapter 5 of his *Guide*.

Another general principle I wish to draw the reader's attention to is the basic pragmatism of Shantideva's teachings. He does not appear to believe in the possibility of one cure or solution to any problem. His is a strategy that involves drawing extensively from all our inner resources. Many of his arguments appeal to what we may call human rationality. But he also uses approaches that appeal to our fundamental humanitarian sentiments. Often he plays upon our sense of moral outrage too. So, the bottom line seems to be "whatever works best." In the final analysis, many of the approaches presented in this book are insights grounded in common sense. For example, who can argue with the sheer practicality of the following lines, which the Dalai Lama is so fond of quoting:

> Why be unhappy about something
> If it can be remedied?
> And what is the use of being unhappy about something
> If it cannot be remedied? (*Guide*, VI:10)

Perhaps most importantly for the modern reader, it is vital to appreciate that both Shantideva and the Dalai Lama do not believe in "instant enlightenment." In their teachings, there is the basic assumption that cultivating inner discipline is a time-consuming process. In fact, the Dalai Lama rightly points out that having expectations of immediate results is a sign of impatience, the very factor the teachings in this volume aim to counteract. With a sense of irony, he observes that often what the modern reader wants is "the best, the fastest, the easiest, and, if possible, the cheapest way." So the journey of someone who is on the path of self-betterment is arduous and requires long commitment. Nevertheless, the rewards of embarking upon such a journey are potentially enormous. Even in immediate terms, the benefit such an endeavor brings to the traveler's life seems remarkable. If the Dalai Lama is representative of those who have gained the fruits of this journey, its merits are shown to be beyond question.

Geshe Thupten Jinpa
Girton College
University of Cambridge

Day One

First Session

Generally speaking, all the major religions of the world emphasize the importance of the practice of love, compassion, and tolerance. This is particularly the case in all the traditions of Buddhism, including the Theravada, Mahayana, and Tantrayana (the esoteric tradition of Buddhism). They all state that compassion and love are the foundation of all the spiritual paths.

In order to enhance one's development of compassion and cultivate the potential for compassion and love inherent within oneself, what is crucial is to counteract their opposing forces. It is in this context that the practice of patience or tolerance becomes very important, because only through patience is one able to overcome the obstacles to compassion.

When we talk about patience or tolerance, we should understand that there are many degrees, starting from a simple tolerance, such as being able to bear a certain amount of heat and cold, progressing toward the highest level of patience, which is the type of patience and tolerance found in the great practitioners, the Bodhisattvas on the high levels of the Buddhist path. Since patience or tolerance comes from a certain ability to remain firm and steadfast, to not be overwhelmed by the adverse situations or conditions that one faces, one should not see tolerance or patience as a sign of weakness, but rather as a sign of strength coming from a deep ability to remain steadfast and firm. We can generally define patience or tolerance in these terms. We find that even in being able to tolerate a certain degree of physical hardship, like a hot or cold climate, our attitude makes a big difference. If we have the realization that tolerating immediate hardship can have long-term beneficial consequences, we are more likely to be able to tolerate everyday hardships. Similarly, in the case of those on the Bodhisattva levels of the path practicing high levels of tolerance and patience, intelligence also plays a very important role as a complementary factor.

In addition to the value of the practice of tolerance and patience from the Dharma point of view, even in our day-to-day life experiences tolerance and patience have great benefits, such as being able to sustain and maintain our calmness of mind, peace of mind, and presence of mind. So if an individual possesses this capacity of tolerance and patience, then even if the person lives in a very tense environment, one that is frantic and stressful, the person's calmness and presence of mind will not be disturbed.

The text from which I am teaching in this series of lectures is a Buddhist text and specifically a text of Mahayana Buddhism. Many of the practices outlined in this work are presented from the point of view of a practitioner who is engaged in the Mahayana path of cultivating bodhichitta and living a way of life according to the Bodhisattva principles. However, many of the techniques and methods which are presented are also relevant and applicable to individuals who do not engage in Bodhisattva practices, or who do not subscribe to Buddhism as a personal religion.

This text is called the *Bodhisattvacharyavatara* in Sanskrit, which is translated as *Guide to the Bodhisattva's Way of Life*. When we speak of the activities of a Bodhisattva, there are three levels. The first is the entry into the Bodhisattva path, which principally involves generating bodhichitta, the altruistic aspiration to attain full enlightenment for the benefit of all sentient beings. That is the first level of practice. This is followed by what is known as the actual practice, which consists of the practice of the six perfections. Among the six perfections, which are the main precepts of generating bodhichitta, one is patience or tolerance. The third level of Bodhisattva deeds comprises the activities at the state of Buddhahood, which results from this practice.

In the first chapter of the *Guide to the Bodhisattva's Way of Life*, Shantideva talks about the merits and benefits of generating bodhichitta, the altruistic aspiration to attain Buddhahood for the benefit of all sentient beings. He states:

> I bow down to the body of him
> In whom the sacred precious mind is born.
> I seek refuge in that source of joy
> Who brings to happiness even those who harm him.
> (*Guide*, I:36)

In this verse, he states that since this altruistic aspiration develops to the infinite capacity of helping all other sentient beings, the person who generates that kind of infinite altruism is truly an object worthy of respect and reverence. Because this infinite altruism is the source of joy and happiness not only for oneself but also for countless other sentient beings, any interaction that other individuals might have with such a person, even a negative one, will leave a very powerful imprint on that individual's life. Even if one commits a negative act or has a negative relationship, although its immediate consequences may be negative, in the long run the very fact that one had an interaction with such a person will lead to positive consequences and benefit in the future. Such is the power of this infinite altruism.

The true foundation of this infinite altruism is compassion, and because compassion is the root of infinite altruism, Chandrakirti—unlike other authors who at the beginning of their text pay homage to the Buddha or a Bodhisattva or a meditational deity—in his text called the *Guide to the Middle Way* pays homage to compassion and points out that its importance and its value remain throughout all time. At the beginner's level, its value cannot be underestimated. While the individual is on the path, the value of compassion and its importance cannot be underestimated. Even at the resultant state of Buddhahood, compassion still retains its importance and value. We find that all major world religions, although they may have different ways of teaching compassion and different ways of explaining why enhancement of a compassionate attitude is important, converge on the single point that compassion is the root. It is crucial.

Compassion can be roughly defined in terms of a state of mind that is nonviolent and nonharming, or nonaggressive. Because of this there is a danger of confusing compassion with attachment and intimacy.

So we find that there are two types of love or compassion. On the one hand is compassion or love which is based on attachment or which is tinged with attachment. That type of love or compassion and feeling of intimacy is quite partial and biased, and it is based very much on the consideration that the object of one's affection or attachment is someone who is dear or close to one. On the other hand, genuine compassion is free from such attachment. There the motivation is not so much that this person is my friend, is dear to me or related to me. Rather, genuine compassion is based on the rationale that just as I do, others also have this innate desire to be happy and overcome suffering; just as I do, they have the natural right to fulfill this fundamental aspiration. Based on that recognition of this fundamental equality and commonality, one develops a sense of affinity and closeness, and based on that, one will generate love and compassion. That is genuine compassion.

It is also very clear that one's level of intelligence or wisdom is a complementary factor that will determine the intensity and the depth of one's compassion. In Buddhism, there are discussions of three principal types of compassion. One is a compassion which is not complemented by any wisdom factors. A second level of compassion is complemented by insight into the transient nature of sentient beings, their impermanent nature. At the third level of compassion, called nonobjectified compassion, the complementary factor is wisdom or insight into the ultimate nature of reality. At this level, one sees the empty nature of sentient beings, and that insight reinforces one's compassionate attitude toward sentient beings. Even though this type of genuine compassion and infinite altruism is something that needs to be consciously cultivated and developed, we all possess the basis or potential for such enhancement and such development.

One of my fundamental beliefs is that not only do we inherently possess this potential or basis for compassion, but also the basic or fundamental human nature is gentleness. Not only human beings but all sentient beings have gentleness as their fundamental nature. There are other grounds upon which I base this belief, without having to resort to the doctrine of Buddha-nature. For example, if we look at the pattern of our existence from an early age until our death, we see the way in which we are so fundamentally nurtured by affection, each other's affection, and how we feel when we are exposed to others' affection. In addition, when we ourselves have affectionate feelings we see how it naturally affects us from within. Not only that, but also being affectionate and being more wholesome in our behavior and thought seems to be much more suited to the physical structure of our body in terms of its effect on our health and physical well-being, and so on. It must also be noted how the contrary seems to be destructive to health. For these reasons I think that we can infer that our fundamental human nature is one of gentleness. Now if this is the case, then it makes all the more sense to try to live a way of life which would be more in accordance with this basic gentle nature of our being.

However, we do find a lot of conflict and tension not only within our individual mind but also within the family, when we interact with other people, and also at the societal level, the national level, the global level, and so on. How do we account for that?

One of the factors, I think, that contributes to this conflict is our imaginative faculty, or in other words, intelligence. It is also our intelligence which can find ways and means to overcome this conflict. So in using human intelligence to overcome this conflict which is created by human intelligence, the important factor is human compassion. I think if we look at the reality, it is quite clear that the best way to overcome conflict is the spirit of reconciliation, even within oneself. That spirit has very much to do with compassion.

One aspect of compassion is to respect others' rights and to respect others' views. That is the basis of reconciliation. I think the rule of the human spirit of reconciliation which is based on compassion is working deep down, whether the person really knows it or not. Therefore, because our basic human nature is gentleness, no matter how much we go through violence and many bad things, ultimately the proper solution is to return to the basic human feeling, that is, human affection. So human affection or compassion is not only a religious matter, but in our day-to-day life it is quite indispensable.

Now with this as a background, if one looks at the practice of tolerance, it is really worthwhile. No matter how difficult, it is worthwhile to do this practice.

The first verse of Shantideva's "Patience" chapter reads:

(1) Whatever wholesome deeds,
Such as venerating the Buddhas and [practicing] generosity,
That have been amassed over a thousand eons,
Will all be destroyed in one moment of anger.

The implication of this first verse is that in order for the individual practitioner to be able to successfully cultivate patience and tolerance, what is required is a very strong enthusiasm, a strong desire, because the stronger one's enthusiasm the greater the ability to withstand the hardships encountered in the process. Not only that, but one also will be prepared to voluntarily accept hardships that are a necessary part of the path.

The first stage, then, is to generate this strong enthusiasm, and for that what is required is to reflect upon the destructive nature of anger and hatred, as well as the positive effects of patience and tolerance.

In this text, one reads that the generation of anger or hatred, even for a single instant, has the capacity to destroy virtues collected over a thousand eons. Another text, the *Entry into the Middle Way* by Chandrakirti, states that a single instant of anger or hatred will destroy virtues accumulated over a hundred eons. The difference between these two texts is explained from the point of view of the object of one's anger or hatred. If the object of one's anger or hatred is a Bodhisattva on a high level of the path, and the person who is being hateful or angry is not a Bodhisattva, then the amount of virtue which will be destroyed is greater. On the other hand, if a Bodhisattva generates anger toward another Bodhisattva, maybe the virtue destroyed would be less. So it is in this regard that the differences are explained.

However, when we say that virtues accumulated over eons are destroyed by a single instant of anger, we have to identify what sort of virtues are destroyed. Both this text and *Entry into the Middle Way* agree that it is only the meritorious virtues, not so much the wisdom aspect but rather the method aspect of the path, which are destroyed. In particular, these include virtues accumulated through practicing giving or generosity as well as virtues accumulated on the basis of observing an ethically disciplined way of life. On the other hand, virtues accumulated through the practice of wisdom, such as generating insight into the ultimate nature of reality, and virtues accumulated through meditative practices, wisdom acquired through meditation, remain beyond the scope of destruction by anger and hatred.

Here there is a mention of the word "eons." A particular Buddhist system of measurement is used here, based on the Abhidharma system, in which "eons" refers to a "great eon," which is composed of twenty middle-length eons. This is also related to Buddhist cosmology, the theory within which the whole evolutionary process of the universe is explained. For instance, according to Abhidharma cosmology, we divide the time of evolution into four stages—the time of empty space, the time of evolution, the time of abiding, and the time of destruction—and all of these are divided according to this precise system. It may be interesting to compare that with the current cosmological theory based on the big bang theory, in which evolution is explained in terms of fifteen to twenty billion years.

According to this verse, the virtues which are complemented by the factor of wisdom, particularly insight into the ultimate nature of reality (the realization of emptiness), and also any virtues which are based on the realization or attainment of *shamatha* (calm abiding or single-pointedness of mind) remain beyond the scope of destruction by anger and hatred. Therefore, we see the value of generating shamatha and insight into emptiness.

The second verse reads:

(2) There is no evil like hatred,
And no fortitude like patience.
Thus I should strive in various ways
To meditate on patience.

Generally speaking, there are many afflictive emotions such as conceit, arrogance, jealousy, desire, lust, closed-mindedness, and so on, but of all these, hatred or anger is singled out as the greatest evil. This is done for two reasons.

One is that hatred or anger is the greatest stumbling block for a practitioner who is aspiring to enhance his or her bodhichitta—altruistic aspiration and a good heart. Anger or hatred is the greatest obstacle to that.

Second, when hatred and anger are generated they have the capacity to destroy one's virtue and calmness of mind. It is due to these reasons that hatred is considered to be the greatest evil.

Hatred is one of the six root afflictive emotions according to Buddhist psychology. The Tibetan word for it is *zhe dang* (Tib. *zhe sdang*), which can be translated as either "anger" or "hatred" in English. However, I feel that it should be translated as "hatred," because "anger," as it is understood in English, can be positive in very special circumstances. These occur when anger is motivated by compassion or when it acts as an impetus or a catalyst for a positive action. In such rare circumstances anger can be positive whereas hatred can never be positive. It is totally negative.

Since hatred is totally negative, it should never be used to translate the Tibetan word *zhe dang* when it appears in the context of tantra. Sometimes we hear the expression "taking hatred into the path." This is a mistranslation. In this context, hatred is not the right word; one should use "anger": "taking anger into the path." So the Tibetan word can be translated as either "anger" or "hatred," but "anger" can be positive; therefore, when *zhe dang* refers to the afflictive emotion it must be translated as "hatred."

The last two lines of the second verse read:

> Thus I should strive in various ways
> To meditate on patience.

Since the goal is the enhancement of one's capacity for tolerance and the practice of patience, what is required is to be able to counteract the forces of anger and hatred, particularly hatred. One should use all sorts of techniques to increase one's familiarity with patience. These include not only real life situations, but also using one's imagination to visualize a situation and then see how one will react and respond to it. Again and again one should try to combat hatred and develop one's capacity for tolerance and patience.

> (3) My mind will not experience peace
> If it fosters painful thoughts of hatred.
> I shall find no joy or happiness;
> Unable to sleep, I shall feel unsettled.

This verse outlines the destructive effects of hatred, which are very visible, very obvious and immediate. For example, when a strong or forceful thought of hatred arises, at that very instant it overwhelms one totally and destroys one's peace and presence of mind. When that hateful thought is harbored inside, it makes one feel tense and uptight, and can cause loss of appetite, leading to loss of sleep, and so forth.

Generally speaking, I believe that the purpose of our existence is to seek happiness and fulfillment. Even from the Buddhist point of view, when we speak of the four factors of happiness, or four factors of fulfillment, the first two are related to the attainment of joy and happiness in worldly terms, leaving aside ultimate religious or spiritual aspirations such as liberation and enlightenment. The first two factors deal with joy and happiness as we understand them conventionally, in worldly terms. In order to more fully experience that level of joy and happiness, the key is one's state of mind. However, there are various factors that contribute to attaining that level of joy and happiness, which we conventionally also recognize as sources of happiness, such as good physical health, which is considered one of the factors necessary for a happy life. Another factor is the wealth that we accumulate. Conventionally, we regard this as a source of joy and happiness. The third factor is to have friends or companions. We conventionally recognize that in order to enjoy a happy and fulfilled life, we also need a circle of friends we trust and with whom we can relate emotionally.

Now all of these are, in reality, sources of happiness, but in order for one to be able to fully utilize them with the goal of enjoying a happy and fulfilled life, one's state of mind is crucial. If one harbors hateful thoughts within, or strong or intense anger somewhere deep down, then it ruins one's health, so it destroys one of the factors. Even if one has wonderful possessions, when one is in an intense moment of anger or hatred, one feels like throwing them—breaking them or throwing them away. So there is no guarantee that wealth alone can give one the joy or fulfillment that one seeks. Similarly, when one is in an intense state of anger or hatred, even a very close friend appears somehow "frosty," cold and distant, or quite annoying.

What this indicates is that our state of mind is crucial in determining whether or not we gain joy and happiness. So leaving aside the perspective of Dharma practice, even in worldly terms, in terms of our enjoying a happy day-to-day existence, the greater the level of calmness of our mind, the greater our peace of mind, and the greater our ability to enjoy a happy and joyful life.

However, when we speak of a calm state of mind or peace of mind, we should not confuse that with a completely insensitive, apathetic state in which there is no feeling, like being "spaced out" or completely empty. That is not what we mean by having a calm state of mind or peace of mind.

Genuine peace of mind is rooted in affection and compassion. There is a very high level of sensitivity and feeling involved. So long as we lack inner discipline, an inner calmness of mind, then no matter what external facilities or conditions we may have, they will never give us the feeling of joy and happiness that we seek. On the other hand, if we possess this inner quality, that is, calmness of mind, a degree of stability within, then even if we lack various external facilities that are normally considered necessary for a happy and joyful life, it is still possible to live a happy and joyful life.

If we examine how anger or hateful thoughts arise in us, we will find that, generally speaking, they arise when we feel hurt, when we feel that we have been unfairly treated by someone against our expectations. If in that instant we examine carefully the way anger arises, there is a sense that it comes as a protector, comes as a friend that would help our battle or in taking revenge against the person who has inflicted harm on us. So the anger or hateful thought that arises appears to come as a shield or a protector. But in reality that is an illusion. It is a very delusory state of mind.

Chandrakirti states in *Entry into the Middle Way* that there might be some justification for responding to force with force if revenge would help one in any way, or prevent or reduce the harm which has already been inflicted. But that is not the case because if the harm, the physical injury or whatever, has been inflicted, it has already taken place. So taking revenge will not in any way reduce or prevent that harm or injury because it has already happened.

On the contrary, if one reacts to a situation in a negative way instead of in a tolerant way, not only is there no immediate benefit, but also a negative attitude and feeling is created which is the seed of one's future downfall. From the Buddhist point of view, the consequence of taking revenge has to be faced by the individual alone in his or her future life. So not only is there no immediate benefit, it is harmful in the long run for the individual.

However, if one has been treated very unfairly and if the situation is left unaddressed, it may have extremely negative consequences for the perpetrator of the crime. Such a situation calls for a strong counteraction. Under such circumstances, it is possible that one can, out of compassion for the perpetrator of the crime and without generating anger or hatred, actually take a strong stand and take strong countermeasures. In fact, one of the precepts of the Bodhisattva vows is to take strong countermeasures when the situation calls for it. If a Bodhisattva doesn't take strong countermeasures when the situation requires, then that constitutes an infraction of one of the vows.

In addition, as the *Entry into the Middle Way* points out, not only does the generation of hateful thoughts lead to undesirable forms of existence in future lives, but also, at the moment that strong feelings of anger arise, no matter how hard one tries to adopt a dignified pose, one's face looks rather ugly. There is an unpleasant expression, and the vibration that the person sends is very hostile. People can sense it, and it is almost as if one can feel steam coming out of that person's body. Indeed not only are human beings capable of sensing it, but pets and other animals also try to avoid that person at that instant.

These are the immediate consequences of hatred. It brings about a very ugly, unpleasant physical transformation of the individual. In addition, when such intense anger and hatred arise, it makes the best part of our brain, which is the ability to judge between right and wrong and assess long-term and short-term consequences, become totally inoperable. It can no longer function. It is almost as if the person had become crazy. These are the negative effects of generating anger and hatred. When we think about these negative and destructive effects of anger and hatred, we realize that it is necessary to distance ourselves from such emotional explosions.

Insofar as the destructive effects of anger and hateful thoughts are concerned, one cannot get protection from wealth; even if one is a millionaire, one is subject to these destructive effects of anger and hatred. Nor can education guarantee that one will be protected from these effects. Similarly, the law cannot guarantee protection. Even nuclear weapons, no matter how sophisticated the defense system may be, cannot give one protection or defend one from these effects.

The only factor that can give refuge or protection from the destructive effects of anger and hatred is the practice of tolerance and patience.

Meditation

Now, let us pause for five minutes of silent meditation, reflecting on what we have discussed so far.

QUESTIONS

Q: When you spoke the other night, I believe you said that our nature was compassionate and gentle.

A: Yes.

Q: Then where does hatred come from?

A: That is a question which requires long hours of discussion. From the Buddhist viewpoint, the simple answer is that it is beginningless. As a further explanation, Buddhists believe that there are many different levels of consciousness. The most subtle consciousness is what we consider the basis of the previous life, this life, and future lives. This subtle consciousness is a transient phenomenon which comes about as a consequence of causes and conditions. Buddhists have concluded that consciousness itself cannot be produced by matter. Therefore, the only alternative is to accept the continuation of consciousness. So that is the basis of the theory of rebirth.

Where there is consciousness, ignorance and hatred also arise naturally. These negative emotions, as well as the positive emotions, occur right from beginningless time. All these are a part of our mind. However, these negative emotions actually are based on ignorance, which has no valid foundation. None of the negative emotions, no matter how powerful, have a solid foundation. On the other hand, the positive emotions, such as compassion or wisdom, have a solid basis: there is a kind of grounding and rootedness in reason and understanding, which is not the case with afflictive emotions like anger and hatred.

The basic nature of the subtle consciousness itself is something neutral. So it is possible to purify or eliminate all of these negative emotions. That basic nature we call Buddha-nature. Hatred and negative emotions are beginningless; they have no beginning, but there is an end. Consciousness itself has no beginning and no end; of this we are certain.

Q: How do we judge when a strong countermeasure is required and what it will be? Please describe what we can learn from your actions in response to the Tibetan genocide.

A: One of the reasons there is a need to adopt a strong countermeasure against someone who harms you is that if you let it pass, there is a danger of that person becoming habituated to extremely negative actions, which in the long run will cause that person's own downfall and is very destructive for the individual himself or herself. Therefore a strong countermeasure, taken out of compassion or a sense of concern for the other, is necessary. When you are motivated by that realization, then there is a sense of concern as part of your motive for taking that strong measure.

In terms of the way we have been dealing with the Chinese government, we have always tried to avoid negative emotions. We consciously make it a point not to let our emotions overwhelm us.

So even if there is a likelihood of some feeling of anger arising, we deliberately check ourselves and try to reduce that, and try to deliberately develop a feeling of compassion toward the Chinese.

One of the reasons why there is some ground to feel compassionate toward a perpetrator of crime or an aggressor is that the aggressor, because he or she is perpetrating a crime, is at the causal stage, accumulating the causes and conditions that later lead to undesirable consequences. So from that point of view, there is enough ground to feel compassionate toward the aggressor.

It is through this type of reflection that we try to deal with the Chinese. And you are right, one can say that this is an example of how one can deal with hatred and aggression. At the same time, we never lose sight of the importance of holding firmly to our own principles and adopting the strong measures that are necessary.

Q: Often when I counteract hatred, even without feeling hatred myself, it seems to increase the other person's hatred. How can I deal with this?

A: I think that is a very good question. In such cases, we have to decide on the spot, according to the situation. This requires sensitivity to the actual context and situation. In some cases, you are right, by taking a strong countermeasure, even without feeling hatred, it might increase the intensity of the other person's feeling of hatred and anger. If that is the case, then perhaps it is possible to let it pass and not take a strong countermeasure.

However, here you have to judge the consequences of your response to a situation. If it is going to make the other person develop a bad habit of repeating the same pattern of action in the future, which will be destructive in the long term, then it may call for a strong countermeasure. But if taking a strong countermeasure will aggravate the situation and increase the other person's anger and hatred, then perhaps what the situation requires is a kind of letting go, letting it pass, and not taking a strong countermeasure. So you need a sensitivity to particular situations.

This is quite analogous to one of the Buddhist principles, which is that, so far as your own personal requirements are concerned, the ideal is to have fewer involvements, fewer obligations, and fewer affairs, businesses, or whatever. However, so far as the interest of the larger community is concerned, you must have as many involvements as possible and as many activities as possible.

Q: Why does anger destroy so much virtue, rather than one moment of anger destroying one equivalent moment of virtue? Is it because it requires eons of virtue to create that moment of happiness, and anger does not permit one to enjoy that moment?

A: It is very difficult to answer this question and say why this is the case. Perhaps these points are what Buddhists would call "extremely hidden phenomena." Generally speaking, when we talk about the nature of reality and the objects of our investigation, Buddhism divides phenomena into three categories. One category includes all the things and events which are obvious, evident to our senses. Then there is a second level of phenomena: things or events which may not seem very obvious or evident, but which you can, through inference, understand or perceive. An example is insight into the nature of emptiness: it is not obvious, but through application of your analytic faculty, you can infer the empty nature of phenomena. Similarly, the transient or impermanent, momentarily changing nature of phenomena is something that you can understand through inference. The third level or category of phenomena is technically called "extremely hidden phenomena."

So regarding questions such as generating anger or hatred toward a Bodhisattva, a single moment of that anger or hatred has the capacity to destroy virtues accumulated over eons. These phenomena are something that one cannot logically understand, or understand through inference; they are not obvious or evident. It is only by relying on the testimony of scriptures that we can accept them. When we talk about relying on testimony, or relying on scriptural authority, not just any scripture will do. Authoritative scriptures must possess certain specific criteria.

At this point, it is important to understand how Buddhists relate to scriptures and scriptural authority of all kinds. Within the Buddhist tradition, there is one school of thought, called the Vaibhashika school, which maintains that so far as the scriptures are concerned, they are the valid teachings of Buddha Shakyamuni, the historical Buddha, and that one can accept them at face value. As a result, for the Vaibhashikas, one cannot make a distinction between definitive scriptures which can be accepted at face value and scriptures which cannot be accepted in this way. However, all the Mahayana schools maintain that one must be able to distinguish between different types of scriptures. Certain scriptures can be accepted at their face value as literal and definitive, whereas other scriptures cannot be accepted as literal and require further interpretation.

So now the question arises, how do we determine that a particular scripture is definitive and literal? If that also requires referring to another scripture, then this process will go on *ad infinitum*, because that also would require another scripture, which would then require another authority, and so on. Ultimately, the authority falls on human reason and understanding. It is through reasoning and understanding that one establishes the difference between a definitive scripture and a nonliteral or interpretable scripture.

Then, if that is the case, how do we determine the validity of a scripture that talks about phenomena which belong to the third category, the extremely hidden phenomena?

Here, as I pointed out earlier, it is only by relying on the authority of the scripture, or the testimony of the Buddha, that one can accept their validity. In order to do that, what is required is to establish the reliability of that teacher, in this case, the Buddha. The way in which we do that is, again, not by referring to a scripture, but rather by examining Buddha's own words, his teachings which deal with the phenomena that one can understand through reason, through inference. These include his presentation of the path, his presentation on the ultimate nature of reality, and so on.

Once you have established the validity of his presentations on these points, then you can develop the conviction of the reliability of the teacher. In addition, one should investigate the specific scripture which presents the extremely hidden phenomena to be sure that there are no internal inconsistencies within the scripture, no contradictions.

So through the combination of these two factors, one finds that the Buddha is a reliable teacher and that the scripture itself has no internal contradiction or inconsistency. Then, you can accept Buddha's testimony on the given issue.

Q: How do we teach patience to our children? How should we react to anger in our children?

A: As to the question of how to teach patience to our children, it is very difficult to explain in words to a child the value of patience and the importance of it. What is crucial here is to set a good example for our children. If you yourself are always short-tempered and lose your temper even at the slightest provocation and then you try to teach children, saying, "Oh, you must be patient, patience is important," it won't have any effect at all.

As to how you should react or respond to anger in children, it is very difficult for me to say, but many of the general principles outlined in the text that teach you how to develop patience would be applicable, even in those circumstances.

Q: What techniques can one use to diffuse anger or hatred when it comes up?

A: What is required here is to judge the situation and figure out what factors have given rise to that particular instance of anger or hatred. Depending on that, you respond, and deal with it accordingly. However, it will also be related to the kind of practices that the individual undertakes in his or her daily life, but this topic will come later in the text.

Q: If there is no extreme form of patience that is a weakness, how can a Bodhisattva take a strong counteraction?

A: There may be a slight misunderstanding of what is meant by a Bodhisattva. One should not have the impression that a Bodhisattva is a very weak person. In fact, Bodhisattvas can be seen as the most courageous beings. They are very determined and firm in their principles. Even conventionally, if people do not tolerate having their toes stepped on and do not tolerate being slighted, if they always take immediate action and stand firm, we consider them courageous and strong, to have strength of character. If that is the case, then Bodhisattvas are beings who have made a pledge or developed the determination that they will combat the evils that exist in the minds of all sentient beings. In a way, that is a kind of arrogance, but it is, of course, based on sound reason. This type of courageous attitude is in some sense arrogant, but not in a negative way.

If we read the aspirational prayers composed by the Bodhisattvas, such as the tenth chapter of the *Guide* to *the Bodhisattva's Way of Life*, the "Dedication" chapter, we find that Bodhisattvas have many aspirations that in reality cannot be realized. Nonetheless, they have this kind of vision and aspiration. So I consider them heroes. I think they are very, very courageous sentient beings. I do not consider this a weakness at all. Bodhisattvas have that kind of outlook, and they are definitely capable of taking strong countermeasures when necessary.

Q: When we dedicate the merit from past practices, is it destroyed by present anger or hatred?

A: If your dedication is complemented by factors of very strong aspiration to attain liberation, or complemented by the factor of bodhichitta, altruistic aspiration, or a realization of the empty nature of phenomena, then, of course, the merit will remain beyond the scope of destruction and will be protected.

Dedication is a very important element of practice in the Buddhist path. We find that in Maitreya's *Ornament of Clear Realizations*, when he outlines the proper manner in which dedication should be practiced, he points out the importance of a strong motivation of bodhichitta. When you dedicate merit, you must have a very strong motivation of bodhichitta, dedicating your merit for the benefit of all sentient beings. In addition, while you do the dedication, you should have clear realization of the empty nature of phenomena, the illusion-like nature of phenomena. Once you have dedicated merit, it should be "sealed" by the recognition that the agent is inherently empty, and that both this very act and the object of your act are also inherently empty. That is what is called "being sealed by the three spheres." So through these practices, you can protect the merit.

In order for one's Dharma practice to be effective and powerful it is not enough to concentrate on one aspect of the practice alone. What is required are many complementary factors, the wisdoms, the dedications, and so on. This is particularly true in the approach of the Mahayana path.

SECOND SESSION

When we talk about friendship, we can generally distinguish two types. Some friendships are not genuine, such as those based on wealth, power, or position. In these cases, friends remain friends so long as the basis on which their friendship is founded is sustained, such as power, wealth, or position. However, once these grounds disappear, then the friendship begins to erode.

On the other hand, we have genuine friendships based on true human feeling, a feeling of closeness in which there is a sense of sharing and connectedness. This type of friendship I would call genuine because it is not affected by the increase or decrease of the individual's wealth, status, or power. The factor that sustains that friendship is whether or not the two people have mutual feelings of love and affection. If love and affection are lacking, then one will not be able to sustain genuine friendship. This is very obvious.

(4) A master who has hatred
Is in danger of being killed
Even by those who for their wealth and happiness
Depend upon his kindness.

(5) By it, friends and relatives are disheartened;
Though drawn by my generosity they will not trust me.
In brief, there is nobody
Who lives happily with anger.

(6) Hence the enemy, anger,
Creates sufferings such as these,
But whoever assiduously overcomes it
Finds happiness now and hereafter.

The sixth verse presents the value and benefits of tolerance and patience. The more one is able to reflect on the destructive effects of anger and hatred as well as the beneficial effects of tolerance and patience, the more one is able to develop a clear recognition of these, the more one will become cautious and distant toward angry and hateful thoughts. Consequently, one will develop an affinity for feelings of tolerance and patience. That, in itself, will have a significant impact upon one's mind. One's enthusiasm for enhancing one's own capacity for tolerance and patience will increase, and likewise one's actual practice of patience will increase as well.

Once one has developed that high level of enthusiasm for the practice, then one should engage in the actual practice itself, that is, enhancing tolerance and patience. The technique which is adopted here is to first seek and examine the causal factors and conditions that give rise to anger and hatred. This is very much in conformity with the general Buddhist approach for dealing with problems and difficult situations.

For example, in Buddhism the principle of causality is accepted as a natural law, and in dealing with reality one has to take that law into account. For instance, in the case of everyday experiences, if there are certain types of events which one does not desire, the best method of ensuring that those events do not take place is to make sure that the causal conditions which normally give rise to them do not occur. Similarly, if one desires a particular event or experience, then the logical thing to do is to seek and accumulate the causes and conditions that would give rise to it.

This is also the case with mental states and experiences. If one desires a particular experience, one should seek the causes that would give rise to it, and if one does not desire a particular experience, like pain or suffering, then one should ensure that the causes and conditions which would give rise to it no longer arise.

An appreciation of this causal principle is very important. Having developed the wish that one would like to reduce one's hatred and anger and overcome them, if one simply wishes or prays that anger and hatred no longer arise, or simply prays that they just disappear, this will not make it happen. In addition, if one tries to do something when hatred or anger has already arisen it is unlikely to have much effect since at that moment one's mind is gripped by the intensity of anger and hatred. At that instant, to try to apply something to prevent that arisal is a bit foolish; one is already almost out of control.

So, the best method is first of all to identify what factors normally give rise to anger and hatred.

(7) Having found its fuel of mental unhappiness
In the prevention of what I wish for
And in the doing of what I do not want,
Hatred increases and then destroys me.

This verse states that the factor that fuels anger or hatred is, in this translation, mental unhappiness, but I think "discontent" may be a better word. A nagging sense of discontent, a feeling of being dissatisfied, or of something being not right, is the fuel that gives rise to anger and hatred. What one should do is try to see how to prevent the arising of that fuel, this feeling of discontent and dissatisfaction. Generally, this discontent arises in us when we feel that either we ourselves, or someone we love, or our close friends are being treated unfairly or threatened: people are being unjust toward us or our close friends. At that instant this feeling of discontent or unhappiness arises. Also, when others somehow obstruct us in achieving something, we feel that we are being trodden upon, and then we feel angry. So the approach here is to get at the root, appreciating the causal nexus, the chain, which would then ultimately explode in an emotional state like anger or hatred. The idea is to stop it at an early stage, rather than wait for that anger or hatred to arise fully. For example, if one wants to stop the flow of a river, the best way is to go to the source and do something about it; either divert it or do something else.

(8) Therefore I should totally eradicate
The fuel of this enemy,
For this enemy has no other function
Than that of causing me harm.

Here the "enemy" is this internal enemy, which is our true enemy, the ultimate enemy: hatred. This feeling of hatred not only destroys our immediate calmness and peace of mind, but also it throws us into a state of confusion. It throws us into a very complicated situation in which we are constantly confronted with confusion, problems, and difficulties.

So what is stated here is that, in fact, hatred, this inner enemy, has no function other than causing us harm. It has no other function than simply destroying us, both in the present and in the future.

This is very different from an ordinary enemy. Although a person whom we regard as an enemy may engage in activities which are harmful to us, at least he or she has other functions: that person has to eat, that person has to sleep. So he or she has many other functions, and therefore cannot devote twenty-four hours a day to this project of destroying us. On the other hand, hatred has no other function, no other purpose, than destroying us. Realizing this fact, one should resolve as a practitioner never to allow an opportunity for this enemy, hatred, to arise.

It is possible that when combating hatred, one might get the idea, "Hatred is an inherent part of my mind. It is part of my psyche. How can I engage in an endeavor where I am trying to combat part of my own mind?" Here, it is useful to know that the human mind is not only complex, but also very skillful. It is capable of finding various ways in which it can deal with difficult situations and different perspectives it can adopt.

For instance, in the Buddhist text called *Ornament of Clear Realizations* there is a particular meditation relating to the First Noble Truth, the truth of suffering, in which one views one's own physical body as an enemy and then engages in a kind of dialogue. Similarly, in the context of practicing bodhichitta, where one enhances one's altruistic attitude, there is also a type of meditation where one engages in a dialogue between one's own self-centered attitude, a self which is the embodiment of self-centeredness, and oneself as a practitioner. Similarly, although hatred and anger are part of one's mind, one can engage in an endeavor in which one takes anger and hatred as objects and combats them.

In addition, in our own daily experience we often find ourselves in situations where we blame ourselves. We say, "Oh, on such and such day, I let myself down." Then one feels angry toward oneself. In reality, there are not two distinct selves; there is just the continuum of one individual. Nonetheless, it makes sense to criticize oneself. There is a kind of dialogue there as well. This is something that we all know from our own experience. Even though in reality there is only one single, individual continuum, there are two different perspectives adopted. When one says, "I did wrong" and "That was not good," one is criticizing oneself. The self which is criticizing is acting from a perspective of oneself as a totality, an entire being, and the self which is being criticized is a self from the perspective of a particular experience or event. So one can see the possibility of having a self-to-self relationship.

It may be helpful here to reflect upon the various aspects of one's own personal identity. Let us take the example of a Tibetan Buddhist monk. That individual can have a sense of personalized identity from the perspective of being a monk, "I, a monk." Then he can also have a level of personal identity which is based not so much upon his consideration of monkhood, but rather on his ethnic origin, Tibetan. So he can say, "I, a Tibetan." Then that person, at another level, can have another identity where monkhood and his ethnic origin may not play any important role. He can think, "I, a human being." So one can see different perspectives within each person's individual identity. What this indicates is that when we conceptually relate to something, we are capable of looking at one phenomenon from many different angles, yet usually we are quite selective. We focus on a particular angle, a particular aspect of that phenomenon, and adopt a particular perspective.

> (9) Whatever befalls me
> I shall not disturb my mental joy;
> For having been made unhappy, I shall not accomplish what
>   I wish
> And my virtues will decline.

The ninth verse indicates that as a practitioner of patience we make a pledge that "whatever befalls me, I shall not allow it to disturb my mental joy."

Mental joy refers to a state of calmness or stability, which is the counterfactor of discontent or mental unhappiness. The reason why one makes the resolve that one will never let one's mental joy be disturbed is because by being unhappy and discontented, one will not be able to accomplish what one wishes. So in a way being unhappy is quite pointless. It is also destructive because losing one's mental joy and mental stability gives rise to situations where one's virtues also decline through the generation of anger and hatred.

(10) Why be unhappy about something
If it can be remedied?
And what is the use of being unhappy about something
If it cannot be remedied?

Here Shantideva gives another reason to avoid becoming unhappy, which is that if the situation or the nature of the problem is such that it can be remedied, then there is no need to be annoyed with it or to be unhappy about it. On the other hand, if the situation is such that the problem or the difficulty has no remedy and no possibility of resolution, then there is also no point in being annoyed with it or unhappy about it.

In the eleventh verse, Shantideva identifies the factors that normally give rise to feelings of discontent and mental unhappiness. It reads:

(11) For myself and for my friends
I want no suffering, no disrespect,
No harsh words and nothing unpleasant;
But for my enemies it is the opposite.

This explains the eight worldly concerns. Generally speaking, a worldly attitude involves feeling happy when certain pleasant things happen, and unhappy when things go wrong. We feel happy when people praise us, and unhappy when people insult or say bad things about us. Likewise, we feel happy when we achieve the material things that we aspire to obtain, and unhappy when these are not achieved. We also feel happy when we become famous, and unhappy when we become notorious. So just as we have these natural feelings in relation to these eight phenomena, we have similar feelings when these events happen to close friends, family members, or someone whom we love.

However, this is not the case when these events happen to our enemy. In the enemy's case, it is the reverse. We feel unhappy when the enemy is having a successful life and happy when the enemy's fortune is declining. We feel quite miserable and unhappy when our enemy become famous, and happy when that fame declines. This is the normal attitude that we have.

What this indicates is that we have a natural tendency to dislike suffering, unhappiness, and problems, and we naturally seek joy, pleasure, and happiness. Since it is in relation to this natural tendency that our feelings of discontent and unhappiness arise, Shantideva points out that our attitude toward suffering may need modification. Suffering may not be as bad as we think.

Consequently, it is important to understand the basic Buddhist stance toward the whole question of suffering. In Buddha's own public teachings, the first thing he taught was the principle of the Four Noble Truths, the first of which is the truth of suffering. In this teaching, he placed a lot of emphasis on realizing the suffering nature of existence. The reason why reflection on suffering is so important is because there is a possible way out, an alternative, which is the possibility of freedom from suffering. It is because of this that the realization of our suffering nature becomes crucial. Otherwise, if there were no hope, no possibility of freedom from suffering, mere reflection on suffering would be a form of morbid thinking and quite negative.

Here, Shantideva encourages us: in order to free ourselves from intense future suffering, he urges us to adopt a certain attitude so that we'll be able to withstand immediate hardships for this higher purpose.

The twelfth verse reads:

> (12) The causes of happiness sometimes occur,
> But the causes for suffering are very many.

While we find that there are many factors and conditions that cause pain and suffering in our lives, the conditions that would give rise to joy and happiness are comparatively rare. Since this is the reality of our existence, it makes more sense to adopt an attitude that will engender a greater degree of tolerance. Suffering is part of our reality, a natural fact of our existence. It is something that we have to undergo, whether we like it or not. We might as well adopt an attitude that enables us to tolerate it so that we are not so intensely affected by it mentally. If we do not have that level of tolerance our life will be miserable. For example, when one has a very bad night, that night seems eternal and never seems to end. Similarly, if one does not adopt an attitude that will enable one to tolerate suffering, then life will become more miserable.

For example, when someone is brought up in a very privileged environment with material abundance and without hardships, that person becomes spoiled, often to the degree that his or her level of tolerance toward difficulties is very low. When even the slightest problem arises, that person cannot handle it. My late elder brother, Lobsang Samten, who spent many years in the United States, once told me that if the electricity goes out and does not come back on for a while, it is possible that many people would die of starvation, because so much is dependent upon electricity. There are freezers, refrigerators, and electric cookers, and so on: the facilities of life are very advanced. In many of the high-rise buildings in cities, there are elevators, and if there is no electricity, the elevators cannot operate. Then people living upstairs either have to prepare themselves for a long meditation or, if it is winter, they may freeze to death.

The last two lines of the twelfth verse read:

> Without suffering there is no renunciation.
> Therefore, mind, you should stand firm.

These two lines tell us that not only is it important to reflect upon suffering, but there is great benefit in doing so as well. Reflecting on suffering has a tremendous significance because only through recognizing the nature of suffering is it possible to generate a genuine sense of renunciation, a genuine desire to seek freedom from this bondage.

For instance, in the case of a practicing Buddhist, one has to reflect not only upon the suffering of immediate and obvious pains, but also upon this very existence as being of the nature of suffering and dissatisfaction. So long as one is under the influence of karma and delusions, one is in a state of suffering and dissatisfaction. So we can perceive the obvious sufferings like pain, hardships, injuries, and so forth, as strong indicators of the basic dissatisfactory nature of our existence. They are like pointers or reminders of this fundamental nature.

Sometimes when I meet practicing Buddhist friends who complain about hardships, pain, suffering, and so forth, I jokingly tell them that in a way one should be grateful for this because ideally we gain experience based on our meditations on suffering. Since that is not happening, the body itself is telling us that we are in this dissatisfactory nature of existence. Therefore, one should be grateful for these pains and sufferings.

> (13) If some ascetics and people of Karnapa
> Endure the pain of cuts and burns for no reason,
> Then for the sake of liberation,
> Why have I no courage?

If people are prepared to put up with hardships, pains, and difficulties in order to obtain goals which are not ultimate, then why should I, who aspire to attain full liberation from suffering, not be able to tolerate a degree of hardship and pain? We can find this instruction in many other Buddhist texts: it is not the way of the wise to give up something great for the purpose of a minor goal; rather it is the way of the wise to give up something minor for a higher purpose or goal. There is a Tibetan expression which says that one should be able to let go of one hundred so that one can get back one thousand. We might think that it is true that one should be able to sacrifice something minor for the sake of a higher purpose, yet still doubt that we have the capacity to actually do that. We might feel disheartened or discouraged.

So in the fourteenth verse, Shantideva says that there is no need to feel disheartened or discouraged because whatever activity it may be, through constant familiarity, through constant training, it is always possible to make something easier and more acceptable. It reads:

(14) There is nothing whatsoever
That is not made easier through acquaintance.
So through becoming acquainted with small harms
I should learn to patiently accept greater harms.

When one is relating to a particular activity or a practice it may seem daunting at the initial stage, but through constant familiarity and through reinforcing one's determination, it is possible to make it easier. It is not that the practice itself has become easier, but rather that one's attitude and one's own mental state have become closer to it. That is why the appearance of the phenomenon has changed.

In the following three verses, Shantideva gives examples of the types of pains and sufferings which one can become accustomed to through familiarity or constant exposure.

(15) Who has not seen this to be so with trifling sufferings,
Such as the bites of snakes and insects,
Feelings of hunger and thirst,
And with such minor things as rashes?

(16) I should not be impatient
With heat and cold, wind and rain,
Sickness, bondage, and beatings;
For if I am, the harm they cause me will increase.

(17) Some when they see their own blood
Become especially brave and steady,
But some when they see the blood of others
Faint and fall unconscious.

Here Shantideva gives examples of two kinds of people: when some see blood, even their own, their courage is increased and they become braver; whereas other people, when they see their own blood or even others' blood, just faint and fall unconscious. This difference comes from conditioning and constant familiarity.

The eighteenth verse begins:

(18) These (reactions) come from the mind
Being either steady or timid.

The next two lines sum up what we were discussing earlier.

Therefore, I should disregard harms caused to me
And not be affected by suffering.

In sum, we have been discussing one of the methods of counteracting the arising of feelings of discontent, dissatisfaction, and mental unhappiness; that is, by bringing about a transformation in our attitude toward suffering and pain. Our normal attitude is the very natural tendency to totally dislike suffering and pain. There is an intensity in our dislike and intolerance of pain and suffering. By contemplating the nature of suffering, and by contemplating the possibility of changing one's attitude through constant familiarity, we reduce that intensity so that our feeling toward suffering is no longer as intolerant as before.

However, I think some of these reflections have to be understood in their proper context. Here, the particular framework of the Buddhist path is more or less presupposed, within which the principles of the Four Noble Truths and the Two Truths are presented. The complete framework includes the ground, path, and resultant state toward which one is heading. Unless one knows the complete context, there is a danger of misunderstanding this type of approach as being rather morbid. So contextualization is crucial.

Therefore, it is very important, whenever one is reading Buddhist texts, that one see what is being presented in its proper context, in relation to other aspects of the Buddhist path. In this regard, I think the Tibetan tradition is admirable because there is always an emphasis on a combined approach of study and practice.

Meditation

During this meditation session, let us focus on the suffering nature of our existence by thinking about momentary change. Momentary change means things are moving and never standing still. In Buddhist practice it is very important to realize that the disintegration of phenomena—events or things—does not require any secondary factor: it is built in as a mechanism. What that indicates is that all things and events are under the power of other factors. When we consider our own body or aggregates, we realize that they are under the influence of the factors of ignorance and delusion. So long as the aggregates remain under the influence of ignorance and delusion, there is no real room for joy or happiness. Ignorance is negative, and anything which remains under the power of a negative force cannot be considered positive or good or desirable.

Hatred, the inner enemy that we have been discussing, and attachment or desire are the two "cronies" of ignorance. In other words, ignorance is like the prime minister or the president. Attachment and hatred are like the two most powerful ministers. Together, they constitute the "three poisons" of mind.

Therefore, the very existence of our life is under the influence of the three poisons. If we are under the power of these three poisonous forces, then certainly our existence is essentially dissatisfactory. So that is the meditation on suffering. That really is the deep root, not just when someone is feeling frustrated about his pains, his body. The main thing is to go to the depths, to get rid of the troublemaker. That is the meditation on suffering.

Begin by thinking of momentary change and its causes, and then consider samsara and its defects. That is the proper way to meditate.

Questions

Q: Western psychotherapy encourages the expression of anger. Is there is an appropriate expression of anger as opposed to the antidote of patience? What do you say to the psychologists and the counselors who say, "Let it all come out," about anger and hatred?

A: Here I think we have to understand that there are many different situations. In some cases, people harbor strong feelings of anger and hurt based on something done to them in the past, an abuse or whatever, and that feeling is kept bottled up. Regarding this, there is a Tibetan expression which says that if there is any sickness in the conch shell, you can clear it by blowing it out. In other words, if anything is blocking the conch shell, just blow it out, and it will be clear. So it is possible to imagine a situation where it may be better to just let out feelings of anger and express them.

However, generally speaking, anger and hatred are the type of emotions which, if left unchecked or unattended, tend to compound themselves and keep on increasing. The more one works with them, the more one adopts a cautious attitude and tries to reduce the level of their force, the better it is.

Q: Aren't hatred and anger connected with attachment, not only toward things, but also principles, ideologies, and especially the identification of "I" as a permanent self?

A: It is very true that both hatred and anger are ultimately rooted in the feeling of a strong, solid notion of self, a permanent ego. Generally speaking, when we talk about grasping at a notion of self or ego, we should distinguish between two types. One definition of ego is a self-centered attitude, where one regards one's own interest as the only one worthy of consideration and remains quite oblivious or indifferent toward others' needs or feelings. Then there is another type of ego, a belief in an enduring, permanent, concrete self or "I." At the beginning stage, these two types of egocentric attitudes are complementary, and one reinforces the other. So, in our minds they are inextricably linked.

But if one emphasizes the practice of bodhichitta, the aspiration to attain Buddhahood for the sake of all sentient beings, and yet harms that altruistic capacity by paying little attention to generating insight into the ultimate nature of reality, then it is possible that in some cases it may remain beyond one's intellectual scope. In such cases, the self-centered attitude based upon selfish thoughts, a feeling of disregard for others' well-being and others' feelings, may decrease, but grasping at a permanent, abiding, or enduring self may still remain. Similarly, if one emphasizes the practice of emptiness but does not pay attention to the bodhichitta aspect of the path, then grasping at a permanent, abiding, concrete self may loosen, but the selfish, self-centered attitude may still remain. So at a higher level, one can see a distinction between these two types of ego.

This is why it is so important when engaging in the spiritual path toward perfection to be able to adopt a path where there is the unification of good method and wisdom, skillful means and insight.

I think this question is also related to the basic Buddhist stance that because hatred and attachment are ultimately rooted in ignorance, in a misconception of the nature of reality, the specific antidotes to anger and hatred and specific antidotes to attachment can be seen as limited because they are specific to individual afflictive emotions. On the other hand, the antidote to ignorance or misconception is more comprehensive in that it serves as an antidote not only to ignorance but also to hatred and attachment because they are rooted in ignorance.

Also, when we talk about the notion of self in Buddhism, it is important to bear in mind that there are different degrees or types. There are some types of sense of self which are not only to be cultivated but also to be reinforced and enhanced. For instance, in order to have a strong determination to seek Buddhahood for the benefit of all sentient beings, one needs a very strong sense of confidence, which is based upon a sense of commitment and courage. This requires a strong sense of self. Unless one has that identity or sense of self, one will not be able to develop the confidence and courage to strongly seek this aim. In addition, the doctrine of Buddha-nature gives us a lot of encouragement and confidence because we realize that there is this potential within us which will allow us to attain the perfection that we are seeking. However, there are different types of sense of self which are rooted in a belief in a permanent, solid, indivisible entity called "self" or "I." There is the belief that there is something very concrete or objective about this entity. This is a false notion of self which must be overcome.

Similarly, within this false notion of self, we can see various levels, various gross forms where there is a naive belief in a permanent, abiding, unchanging self. If we go further we find that there is a belief in something possessing a sort of intrinsic reality and a status which is independent and unique to the thing. Again, that is a false notion.

Another strong sense of self which is false involves a tendency to disregard others' well-being and others' feelings and rights. That sense of self is, again, to be discarded and overcome. So we should be very sensitive when we use the words "ego" and "self" in the Buddhist context, not to totally adopt a black-and-white stance saying, "This is out, and this is in."

Q: What is the role of wrathful deities?

A: This is not easy to explain. I think the basic philosophy is that human emotions, such as anger, usually act as a force to bring about swift action. I think that is the foundation. So the general principle behind the idea of wrathful deities is that the one thing which is unique to emotional states such as anger or other afflictive emotions is that they have a kind of energy, and when one experiences that emotional state, there is a kind of energy which would enable the individual to take swift action. It is a very powerful motivating factor. It is in relation to this fact that the practice of relating to wrathful deities has to be understood.

Another thing we have to understand is the basic Buddhist stance toward these so-called afflictive emotions. From the perspective of non-Mahayana systems, since the ultimate goal is one's own personal liberation from samsara, and there is no talk about the importance of generating bodhichitta, all the negative actions of body, speech, and mind are to be abandoned. There are no exceptional circumstances where they are permissible. So they are to be abandoned. Period.

However, in the Mahayana sutra vehicle, because the primary aim of a Bodhisattva practitioner is to be of service to others, there are certain exceptions allowed in regard to the negative actions of body and speech. However, no exceptions are allowed in regard to the nonvirtues of the mind because there is no possibility of mental nonvirtues being beneficial. In the case of the Bodhisattva practitioner, if the situation is such that it is beneficial to the larger community or many sentient beings, then there is permission for the Bodhisattva to use attachment, not so much on the path but as a complementary factor to the path, as an aid toward the goal of helping others. However, there is no permission given to the Bodhisattva for generating hatred or anger in Sutrayana.

Tantric Buddhism contains unique techniques of meditation on emptiness which are based upon deity yoga, the meditative procedure whereby one dissolves ordinary perception and ordinary apprehension and deliberately adopts an identity which is perfected and divine. On that basis, exceptions are also allowed in regard to the use of anger on the path, and it is in this context that the wrathful deities are used in tantric meditation.

Naturally, when one utilizes the energy of anger for the benefit of others, at that time it is much easier to visualize wrathful deities rather than peaceful deities.

Q: If there is no soul, what is the nature of the mindstream that reincarnates from lifetime to lifetime? How can such a consciousness become a separate entity?

A: Once again, it depends very much on how one understands the term "soul." If one understands the term "soul" as a continuum of individuality from moment to moment, from lifetime to lifetime, then one can say that Buddhism also accepts a concept of soul; there is a kind of continuum of consciousness. From that point of view, the debate on whether or not there is a soul becomes strictly semantic. However, in the Buddhist doctrine of selflessness, or "no soul" theory, the understanding is that there is no eternal, unchanging, abiding, permanent self called "soul." That is what is being denied in Buddhism.

Buddhism does not deny the continuum of consciousness. Because of this, we find some Tibetan scholars, such as the Sakya master Rendawa, who accept that there is such a thing as self or soul, the "kangsak ki dak" (Tib. *gang zag gi bdag*). However, the same word, the "kangsak ki dak," the self, or person, or personal self, or identity, is at the same time denied by many other scholars.

We find diverse opinions, even among Buddhist scholars, as to what exactly the nature of self is, what exactly that thing or entity is that continues from one moment to the next moment, from one lifetime to the next lifetime. Some try to locate it within the aggregates, the composite of body and mind. Some explain it in terms of a designation based on the body and mind composite, and so on.

We also find a particular school within the Mahayana tradition called the Chittamatra or Yogachara school, the "Mind-Only" school. One of the divisions of that school maintains that there is a special continuum of consciousness called *alayavijnana*, which is the fundamental consciousness. The reason for positing this is that they feel that if there is such a thing as a self, a stream of consciousness continuing from one lifetime to another, then when we search for the true referent behind the term "self," or "I," or whatever one calls it, it must be findable because if we can't find it then we will be tending towards nihilism. However if we posit a self, or an agent independent of body and mind, then we will be tending toward the extreme of absolutism. Further, if we were to identify the self or the person from within the stream of consciousness itself, this would be problematic because Buddhism accepts certain states of existence where there is an absence of consciousness, and at that instant there would not be any thought or consciousness present in the mind of the person. So because of these problems, this particular school posits a separate continuum of consciousness called alayavijnana, which is like a fundamental basis.

In addition, one of the reasons the Chittamatrins felt the need to posit this particular type of stream of consciousness is because if we try to explain selfhood or personhood only within the context of six types of consciousness and five sensory faculties, then, as I pointed out earlier, there are problems. For instance, at the stage of thoughtlessness, there is no consciousness; therefore there would not be any person. Similarly, in Buddhism, there is the acceptance of a state of intuitive direct realization of emptiness, when the consciousness has become totally unalloyed, pure, and untainted. At that very instant, even though the person is not fully enlightened, there is no tainted or polluted consciousness. However, one has to accept some form of defilement that would obstruct the person's full enlightenment, and that has to be understood in terms of imprints or dispositions, and so on. Again, because of this, the Chittamatrins found the need to posit this fundamental basis, defined in terms of a neutral consciousness that serves only as a kind of depository of all the various imprints that are implanted in one's psyche.

Q: The societal result of anger and hatred is cold-blooded murder by younger and younger people. What is society's role in responding to the results of anger and hatred?

A: As I pointed out at the press conference yesterday, I feel that there has been negligence over a certain period of time, several decades, during which we did not pay enough attention to the importance of some of the fundamental human values, and that, combined with other factors, has led to the kind of society that we find ourselves in now. Therefore, it is very difficult to come up with simple solutions, just like that. What is required here is a concerted effort from many different angles to try to tackle this problem. Education, no doubt, is one major factor. The way we educate children is very important. I also believe that a teacher's behavior is a very important factor. A teacher's duty is not only to give information or knowledge, but also to set a good example of the principles that we are trying to teach. So the manner in which children are educated becomes very important, particularly by adults setting a good example. In that way, these principles or values become something very dear to the heart of the children. Of course, the media are also very much involved.

Q: What can we do to reduce the influence of greed?

A: In some sense, without greed there would not be any rebirth. In order to have reincarnation, we need greed. As is the case with anger, I think there are different types of greed, some of which can be positive, some negative. Greed is a form of desire. However, it is an exaggerated form of desire, based on overexpectation.

The true antidote of greed is contentment. For a practicing Buddhist, for a Dharma practitioner, many practices can act as a kind of counterforce to greed: the realization of the value of seeking liberation or freedom from suffering, recognizing the underlying unsatisfactory nature of one's existence, and so on. These views also help an individual to counteract greed. But in terms of an immediate response to greed, one way is to reflect upon the excesses of greed, what it does to one as an individual, where it leads. Greed leads one to a feeling of frustration, disappointment, a lot of confusion, and a lot of problems.

When it comes to dealing with greed, one thing which is quite characteristic is that although it arises from the desire to obtain something, it is not satisfied by obtaining it. Therefore, it becomes limitless or boundless, and that leads to trouble. The interesting thing about greed is that although the underlying motive is to seek satisfaction, as I pointed out, even after obtaining the object of one's desire, one is still not satisfied. On the other hand, if one has a strong sense of contentment, it doesn't matter whether one obtains the object or not; either way, one is still content.

Q: What is the relationship between mindfulness and patience and between humility and patience?

A: Generally speaking, when one engages in any form of practice, the habit of mindfulness is necessary because it is defined as a faculty that allows one to maintain attention on an object of observation. Be it patience or other forms of practice, one has to direct one's attention toward that particular practice, so mindfulness is necessary.

There is also a very close connection between humility and patience, because what I meant by generating humility is that although one has the capacity to retaliate, one has decided not to do so. One has the capacity, if one wishes, to take a more confrontational or aggressive stance, and although one has this capacity, one deliberately decides not to do so. That is what I would call a genuine humility. When there is a feeling of helplessness or incapacitation toward the human situation, I wouldn't call that genuine humility, because there is no alternative but to give in.

Similarly, in the case of tolerance or patience, there could be different types. One is genuine and involves the decision to be more tolerant through self-discipline. On the other hand, when one is forced to adopt a response, that would be in some sense meekness rather than tolerance. So again, there are differences.

Generally, tolerance requires self-discipline, the realization that one could have acted otherwise, could have adopted an aggressive approach but has decided not to do so, not that someone forced one to adopt a tolerant attitude. Our practice of tolerance toward the Chinese is genuine, not questionable.

Day Two

First Session

In the *Pratimoksha-sutra*, the scripture on ethics and monastic discipline, Buddha states that one should not indulge in any actions which are unwholesome, but rather should always perform deeds which are wholesome. That way of life should be based on a disciplined state of mind. One should therefore tame or discipline one's mind, and that disciplining, bringing about inner transformation, is indeed the essence of Buddha's doctrine or teaching. So what this indicates is that, ultimately, whether one's action is wholesome or unwholesome depends upon whether that action is arising from a disciplined state of mind or an undisciplined state of mind.

Similarly, we also find in other scriptures statements indicating that if one's mind is disciplined and tamed, or at peace, then it will lead to joy and happiness, whereas if one's mind is undisciplined and not at peace, then it will lead to unhappiness and suffering. Ultimately it is one's state of mind which is the determining factor.

In general, it is possible to indicate one's particular spiritual way of life through external means, such as wearing certain clothes, having a shrine or altar in one's house, doing recitations and chanting, and so on. However, these practices or activities are secondary to one's religious or spiritual way of life because all of these activities can be performed by a person who harbors a very negative state of mind. On the other hand, all the virtues of mind, the mental qualities, are genuine Dharma or genuine spiritual qualities because all of these internal mental qualities cannot exist in a single moment simultaneously with ill feelings or negative states of mind.

So engaging in training or a method of bringing about inner discipline within one's mind is the essence of a religious life. Whether or not one leads a spiritual life depends on whether or not one has been successful in bringing about that disciplined, tamed state of mind.

As far as the actual techniques for bringing about that internal transformation are concerned, the basic approach that is employed in the Buddhist path is a unification of skillful means, or method, and wisdom. For example, let us take the case of the particular text that we are dealing with, the *Guide to the Bodhisattva's Way of Life* by Shantideva. In this text, the ninth chapter deals with the wisdom aspect of the path, that is, generating insight, whereas the remaining chapters all deal with the method aspect, the skillful means of the path. So when we speak about skillful means or the method aspect of the Mahayana path, the principal practice is the development of love and compassion. In order to successfully enhance these qualities of love and compassion, one must be able to counteract the factors which obstruct one's cultivation of these qualities. In this regard the practice of tolerance and patience becomes crucial for Bodhisattva practitioners.

Just as in the general path of Mahayana Buddhism, where the method and the wisdom aspects of the path complement and reinforce each other, here the practice of tolerance and patience is necessary for generating and enhancing one's capacity for love and compassion. As one progresses on the path, love and compassion on the one hand, and patience and tolerance on the other, become complementary and reinforce each other.

The next two verses read:

(19) Even when the wise are suffering
Their minds remain very lucid and undefiled;
For when war is being waged against the disturbing
   conceptions
Much harm is caused at the time of battle.

(20) The victorious warriors are those
Who, having disregarded all suffering,
Vanquish the foes of hatred and so forth;
(Common warriors) slay only corpses.

When we are engaged in the practice of patience and tolerance, in reality what is happening is that we are engaged in combat with hatred and anger. Since it is a situation of combat, one seeks victory, but one also has to be prepared for the possibility of losing the battle. So while one is engaged in combat, one should not lose sight of the fact that in the process one will encounter many problems and hardships. One should have the ability to withstand these hardships and have the fortitude to bear these problems. Someone who gains victory over hatred and anger through such an arduous process is a true hero. On the other hand, those people who fight with other human beings out of anger, hatred, and strong emotion, even if they gain victory over their enemies in battle, are not in reality true heroes. What they are doing is slaying corpses, because human beings, being transient, will die. Whether or not these enemies die in the battle is another question, but they will die at some point. So what is happening, in reality, is that they are slaying corpses. The true hero is the one who gains victory over hatred and anger.

One might feel that while it is true that one should engage in combat with hatred and anger and other delusions, what guarantee do we have, what assurance do we have, that we can gain victory over them? I think this point is very important. One must have some assurance that one can, if one energetically pursues it, gain victory over the delusions.

If we pay enough attention, it is quite simple to recognize these afflictive emotions and thoughts, called *nyon mongs* in Tibetan, which literally means "that which afflicts the mind from within." The term is often translated simply as "delusions." The etymology of the Tibetan word gives one a sense that they are emotional and cognitive events. They automatically afflict one's mind; they destroy one's peace of mind and bring about a disturbance within one's psyche. It is quite obvious that if we pay enough attention, we will be able to realize their afflictive nature when they arise, because they have a tendency to destroy our calmness and presence of mind. But what is difficult is to discover whether, through applying the corresponding antidotes, we can overcome and eliminate them or not. That is a question that directly relates to the whole idea of whether or not it is possible to attain nirvana or liberation from samsara. That is a very serious and difficult question.

So far as the Buddhist concept of nirvana, that is, liberation or freedom, is concerned, we find its earliest discussion in the scriptures belonging to the first public discourse that the Buddha gave, which principally deals with the Four Noble Truths. But full and comprehensive understanding of nirvana and liberation can be developed only on the basis of understanding the teachings presented in the second and third public discourses.

So what premises or grounds do we have for accepting that these mental afflictions can be ultimately rooted out and eliminated from our mind? In Buddhist thought, we have three principal reasons for believing that this can happen. One is that all deluded states of mind, all afflictive emotions and thoughts, are essentially distorted in their mode of apprehension, whereas all the antidotal factors such as love, compassion, insight, and so on not only are undistorted, but they also have grounding in our varied experience and in reality.

Second, all these antidotal forces also have the quality of being strengthened through practice and training. Through constant familiarity, one can enhance their capacity and increase their potential limitlessly. So the second premise is that as one enhances the capacity of these antidotal forces and increases their strength, one is able to correspondingly reduce the influences and effects of delusory states of mind.

The third premise is that the essential nature of mind is pure; in other words, there is the idea that the essential nature of mind is clear light or Buddha-nature.

So it is on these three premises that Buddhism accepts that

delusions, all afflictive emotions and thoughts, can be ultimately eliminated through practice and meditation.

Some of these points are quite obvious, so that if one just pays enough attention they will become quite clear, while some may remain quite obscure or hidden. However, through analysis and investigation, one will be able to develop inferences, so all of these can be understood through investigation and analysis. They do not require accepting the testimony of a scriptural authority.

One of the reasons that Buddha's words can be accepted as valid in relation to very obscure phenomena is that in regard to less hidden things his teachings have proven to be reliable and valid. The principal concern of a seeker is to find out whether or not it is possible to attain liberation or freedom from suffering. And so far as that subject is concerned, Buddha's teachings have been proven to be valid and reliable.

(21) Furthermore, suffering has good qualities:
Through being disheartened with it, arrogance is dispelled,
Compassion arises for those in cyclic existence,
Evil is shunned, and joy is found in virtue.

In this verse, Shantideva elaborates on the benefits of thinking about suffering. First, he states that when one reflects upon suffering, when one appreciates the underlying unsatisfactory nature of our existence, then it will automatically reduce one's arrogance and feeling of conceit. Additionally, when one is aware of this suffering nature and of one's own pains and suffering, it also helps one to develop a capacity for empathy, the capacity which allows one to connect with other people's feeling and suffering, thereby enhancing one's capacity for compassion toward others. In addition, by realizing the nature of suffering one will develop greater resolve to put an end to the unwholesome deeds which lead to suffering, and one's enthusiasm for engaging in wholesome actions and deeds which lead to happiness and joy will increase. So these are the benefits or merits of thinking about suffering.

However, it is important to be very skillful in one's application of the various techniques, and not to be extreme in one's approach. For instance, if we have too much self-importance, if we are puffed up by arrogance based on our supposed or actual achievements or qualities, then the antidote is to think more about suffering and one's own problems and the unsatisfactory nature of existence. This will assist in bringing down the level of one's high opinion of oneself; it will bring one more down to earth, as it were.

On the other hand, if one finds that by reflecting on the unsatisfactory nature of existence, suffering, pain, and so forth, one feels quite overwhelmed, then there is again a danger of going to the other extreme, where one might become totally discouraged, helpless, and depressed. This can lead to thinking, "Oh, I can't do anything, I'm not worth anything." That extreme is another danger. So under such circumstances, it is important to be able to uplift one's mind by reflecting on one's achievements, the progress that one has made so far, one's other positive qualities, and so on, so that one can get out of that discouraged or demoralized state of mind. What is required here is a balanced and skillful approach.

This is analogous to planting a sapling or a seedling. At its very early stage, one has to be very skillful and gentle: too much moisture will destroy it, too much sunlight will destroy it. What one needs is a balanced environment where the sapling can have healthy growth. Similarly, what one is seeking here is healthy emotional and psychological growth. So here again one needs that gentle and skillful approach, otherwise there is a danger of going to extremes.

It also can happen that someone just picks out a passage from a Buddhist text and says, "This is the Buddhist approach." The tendency to look at Buddhist techniques in black-and-white terms, as if one particular technique is applicable everywhere, universally, without any qualification, must be avoided.

In other words, the real practice of Dharma is in some ways like a voltage stabilizer. When there is a power surge, the function of the stabilizer is to provide stable and constant power.

(22) As I do not become angry
With great sources of suffering such as jaundice,
Then why be angry with animate creatures?
They too are provoked by conditions.

(23) Although they are not wished for,
These sicknesses arise;
And likewise although they are not wished for,
These disturbing conceptions forcibly arise.

(24) Without thinking, "I shall be angry,"
People become angry with no resistance,
And without thinking, "I shall produce myself,"
Likewise anger itself is produced.

In the twenty-second verse, Shantideva presents a technique of developing patience or tolerance based on an appreciation of the complex reality of a given situation. Here, one can feel that since the aggressor has inflicted this pain and injury on me, I am totally justified in being intolerant. I am totally justified in being hateful or angry toward that person.

Shantideva responds by stating that if we examine this carefully, we will find that among the factors that give rise to our pain and suffering, our feelings of hurt and harm, there are both animate and inanimate factors. Why is it that we particularly hold the animate factors, like people, responsible and accountable, but not the inanimate factors, such as the conditions that give rise to it? For instance, we don't hold grudges against our illnesses, although illness gives us pain.

One could argue that this is quite different, because in the case of inanimate factors such as illnesses, they have no desire to injure us—it's not deliberate. Further, the illnesses and these factors arise without their own deliberation, without their own choice.

Shantideva responds to this by saying that if this is the case, then even when a person inflicts harm on us, the harm that is inflicted is in some sense out of that person's control because he or she is compelled by other forces such as negative emotions, delusions, ill feelings, and so on. If we go even further, we find that even a very negative feeling such as ill will or hatred also comes about as a result of many factors and is the aggregation of many conditions which do not arise out of choice or deliberately.

In the twenty-fifth and twenty-sixth verses, he sums up the reflections that he has outlined earlier, stating that:

> (25) All mistakes that are
> And all the various kinds of evil
> Arise through the force of conditions:
> They do not govern themselves.

> (26) These conditions that assemble together
> Have no intention to produce anything,
> And neither does their product
> Have the intention to be produced.

Again, there is a kind of chain, a causal nexus, one factor leading to another. Nothing has any independent status, nothing has control over itself.

> (27) That which is asserted as Primal Substance
> And that which is imputed as a Self,
> (Since they are unproduced) do not arise after having
>   purposefully thought,
> "I shall arise (in order to cause harm)."

In verse 27, we find a refutation of certain views held by non-Buddhist schools of Shantideva's time, particularly the views of two principal schools, the Samkhya school and the Naiyayika school. The idea that is being presented here is that no things and events arise out of their own choice; none enjoys an independent status. So in order to fully argue for that, one has to anticipate other rival theories having a view or a position that there are certain types of events and things which can enjoy this independent status. Of the two examples which I have given here, the first is the Samkhya theory of *prakriti*, which is a belief in some kind of primary substance. Prakriti is described as the underlying substratum from which arises the whole phenomenal world, as if this primal substance were the essence that creates the entire phenomenal world. The substance itself is independent, eternal, and absolute. The Naiyayika school maintains that "self" similarly enjoys this independent, absolute, eternal sort of status.

(28) If they are unproduced and non-existent
Then whatever wish they have to produce (harm will also
    not exist).
Since (this Self) would permanently apprehend its objects,
It follows that it would never cease to do so.

(29) Furthermore if the Self were permanent
It would clearly be devoid of action, like space.
So even if it met with other conditions
How could its unchanging (nature) be affected?

(30) Even if when acted upon (by other conditions) it
    remains as before,
Then what could actions do to it?
Thus if I say that this (condition) acts upon (a permanent
    Self)
How could the two ever be (causally) related?

In verses 27, 28, 29, and 30, Shantideva refutes these views by drawing extensively on the Buddhist doctrine of universal causation, which asks: If the primal substance or self is permanent and eternal, how can one account for its interaction with the phenomenal world? What is the nature of their relationship? How can one explain conditionality on the basis of the relationship between the phenomenal world and this eternal substance or self? Because if the self or the primal substance is permanent, unchanging, eternal, how can it produce anything? In order for something to have the capacity to produce something, it must itself be a product; it itself must also depend upon other conditions and factors. If it is not produced, it cannot produce any other thing. So it is on the grounds of Buddhist universal causation that these two views are refuted.

In verse 31, Shantideva provides a summary:

(31) Hence, everything is governed by other factors (which
    in turn) are governed by (others),
And in this way nothing governs itself.
Having understood this, I should not become angry
With phenomena that are like apparitions.

The reason the analogy of apparitions is used here is that an apparition is an illusion created by a magician; it has no objective status of its own and is entirely dependent upon the whim of the magician. So there is no objective or independent life of its own; it is created by another factor. Similarly, all phenomena, because they are governed by other factors and come into existence as a result of other causes and conditions, do not enjoy any independent status of their own. From that point of view, they are like apparitions. Therefore, it is inappropriate to respond with such extremes to conditions that do not arise of their own accord because they are, in some sense, quite helpless.

It is important to understand the Buddhist doctrine of universal causality or causation, and when we talk about the principle of causation we have to understand the basic characteristics of this doctrine. It is very clearly presented in Asanga's text called *Compendium of Knowledge*, in which he states that the Buddhist doctrine of causality has three principal characteristics: first, there is no acceptance of an autonomous creator. There is no idea of a design, because Buddha himself states that because the causes were there, the effects, or fruits, followed. So it has to be understood purely in terms of conditionality, because there is no acceptance of an independent autonomous agent or a creator. In sutra, it states, "Because this was produced, it led to this effect." This is the second characteristic—anything that is a cause must itself be of a transient nature; it must be impermanent. If it is permanent, if it is eternal and unchanging, then it cannot have the capacity to produce anything. The third characteristic is that there must be a correspondence, a unique relationship between the cause and the effect. These are the three characteristics of the Buddhist theory of universal causality or the principle of causality.

When the principle of causality is examined further, Buddhism explains two principal types of causes. One is called the "substantial cause," the material that turns into the effect. Then there are contributing causes, which are not primary because they are the factors that assist in turning that material substance into that effect. For example, in the case of a sprout, the water, the temperature, and the fertilizers, and so on are contributing causes. One thing we must bear in mind is that the perspectives adopted here are from the point of view of Mahayana Buddhism and particularly that of the Prasangika Madhyamika. So far as his philosophical position on emptiness is concerned, Shantideva shares the view of Chandrakirti. Both agree in their interpretation of Nagarjuna's philosophy of emptiness; they subscribe to the philosophical tenets of Prasangika Madhyamika. So when we talk of all things and events as being apparitions or illusion-like, we have to understand it from that perspective.

A question is raised here that if all things and events are like apparitions, then why should we take them seriously? Why should they affect us so much? Shantideva responds by saying that although all things and events are like apparitions, the agent or the subject who is undergoing this experience is also like an apparition. However, our own experience of pain and suffering, no matter how apparition-like, is very real. Our own experience affirms their reality—let's not deny that. We face the problem, we undergo suffering, and so far as the reality or the concreteness of their existence is concerned, our experience speaks out. There is no point in denying this. Therefore, just as in a dream, an apparition-like agent can go through suffering and pain, which is also like an apparition. However, one cannot ignore the effects of that reality because our experience affirms its existence. So it is true that by appreciating the apparition-like nature of things and events we can better deal with the problem.

The next verses read:

> (32) —(If everything is unreal like an apparition) then who
> is there to restrain what (anger)?
> Surely (in this case) restraint would be inappropriate.
> It would not be inappropriate, because (conventionally)
> I must maintain
> That in dependence on restraining (anger) the stream of
> suffering is severed.

> (33) So when seeing a human enemy or even a friend
> Committing an improper action,
> By thinking that such things arise from conditions
> I shall remain in a happy frame of mind.

As far as the philosophy of emptiness is concerned, it is extensively presented in the ninth chapter of Shantideva's text.

Meditation

Let us do a meditation with a little bit of visualization. Imagine a scenario where someone that you know very well, someone who is close or dear to you loses his or her temper, either in a very acrimonious relationship, or in a situation where something else is happening. This person shows all signs of being in an intense state of anger or hatred, loses all mental composure, creates very negative "vibes," even goes to the extent of harming himself or herself and breaking things. Then reflect upon the immediate effects of intense anger or hatred. The reason why I think we should visualize this happening to others is because it is easier to see the faults of others than to see our own faults. So visualize this, and even see a physical transformation happening to that person. This person whom you feel close to, whom you like, the very sight of whom gave you pleasure in the past, now turns into this ugly, ugly person, even physically speaking. This is a kind of analytic meditation, so do this meditation and visualization for a few minutes, in an analytical way, using your imaginative faculty. At the end of it, relate that to your own experience. Then resolve, "I shall never let myself fall under the sway of such intense anger and hatred. Because if I do that, I will also be in the same position and suffer all these consequences—lose my peace of mind, lose my composure, assume this ugly physical appearance, and so on." Make that decision, and then remain in an absorptive meditation on this conclusion.

So the first part is an analytic meditation, and the second stage is an absorptive meditation.

If one can use one's imaginative faculty and do this visualization practice, it can be a very powerful and very effective tool. For instance, in our day-to-day life we are exposed to many events and scenarios, like television, films, and so on, in which there are scenes of violence and sex, but it is possible to view them with an underlying mindfulness of the effects of extremes, and, instead of being totally overwhelmed by the sight, you can take these scenes as a kind of indicator from which you can learn lessons. One of the Tibetan Kadampa masters, Potowa, said that for a meditator who has a certain degree of inner stability and realization, every experience comes as a teaching; every event, every experience one is exposed to comes as a kind of learning experience. I think this is very true.

QUESTIONS

Q: Your Holiness, how can we balance our concern for the interests of others with the need to cultivate our own inner qualities?

A: In terms of sequence, one has to take care of one's own inner development first. This is also the principle behind the *Lam Rim* approach of the three scopes, or three capacities. In this approach, practice is graded into three stages, according to the motivation of the individual. Each corresponds to a particular stage in the individual's spiritual development. Even Buddha himself, when he gave public teachings or sermons, did not begin with the teachings on bodhichitta. Rather he began with the teachings on the Four Noble Truths. When he gave the second public discourse, or turning of the wheel of the Dharma, it was then that he spoke extensively about bodhichitta. However, so far as the second and the third public discourses are concerned, it seems there is no historical record of a chronological event; these teachings might have been given to an audience of a select few.

Q: Are all vices only mental habits, and by applying the antidotes for each, are they eliminated, or is this only the method aspect, and must it be used in conjunction with discovering the inherent emptiness of existence?

A: As to your first question, if we examine the nature of our mental afflictions in their present state, all of these cognitive and emotional states are the results or products of their previous instance. There is a kind of continuum. One can therefore say that they are products of conditioning. From the Buddhist point of view, that conditioning factor has to be understood not only within a single lifetime, but it also has to be traced to previous lifetimes; that is, the rebirth theory has to be taken into account. However, external or circumstantial conditioning would also make a difference as to the intensity and degree of the particular afflictive emotion. For instance we find that even within one family, different children of the same parents each have their own natural tendencies, which are products of their previous karma. As they grow up, due to external conditioning and circumstances, certain types of emotions will become stronger and others weaker, and so on. So although the emotional afflictions are the results of conditioning from previous lives and previous instances, there is also an aspect of immediate or circumstantial conditioning as well.

As to the question of how our mental afflictions originate, from the Buddhist point of view one has to accept the Buddha's explanation in terms of the beginninglessness of consciousness. When talking about the beginninglessness of consciousness, I don't personally think that there is a possibility of coming up with an affirmative argument or reason. Although one can explain it on the basis of tracing the substantial continuum of consciousness, I don't think one can come up with a one hundred percent affirmative proof in the sense of a logical deduction. However, the strongest argument is that if we adopt a contrary position, which is that there is a beginning, then we have to accept that either there is an external creator, an agent, which also leads to problems, or we have to accept some type of uncaused event, one which has no cause and conditions. Again, that is logically incoherent and inconsistent.

So given the choice, the position that the continuum of consciousness is beginningless seems to have fewer logical inconsistencies and contradictions. It is on that basis that we will also have to accept the origin of our negative tendencies. We cannot posit a beginning to these habits or tendencies.

However, it is also possible for some individuals to have a high spiritual faculty or heightened consciousness enabling them to look into their past lives, not necessarily to beginningless time, but several lifetimes. That is possible.

As far as the second part of your question is concerned, there seems to be a consensus among all Buddhist traditions that so far as the actual elimination of the afflictive emotions and cognitive events is concerned, the application of wisdom is necessary; it is indispensable. For example, even from the perspective of a tradition which does not subscribe to the philosophy of emptiness, or identitylessness of phenomena, meditating on love and compassion can act as a direct antidote to anger and hatred. However, it would not eliminate or eradicate them completely. In order for that to be done, one needs to employ the faculty of wisdom, a realization of the identitylessness of a person, or selflessness. The consensus among all Buddhist traditions seems to be that there is a need to apply the wisdom factor in order to root out these negative tendencies. In the Mahayana traditions, this is very clear. In both the Yogachara (Mind-Only) school and the Madhyamika (Middle Way) school, the eradication of both obstructions, i.e., afflictions of the mind and obstructions to knowledge, can be achieved only through generating insight into the nature of emptiness, or selflessness.

So insight into selflessness is seen as the direct antidote to delusions, or afflictive emotions and cognitive events, and insight into the ultimate nature of reality or the ultimate emptiness of phenomena is seen as the direct antidote that would root out the imprints and the residual potencies that are implanted in one's psyche by the delusions.

However, according to the Prasangika Madhyamika school, the identitylessness of persons and the identitylessness of phenomena are understood only in relation to the subject or object which they qualify; there is no difference in terms of their negation. Again, it is only by generating insight into the nature of emptiness that one can cut the root of afflictive emotions and thoughts.

Q: In what ways do the images in dreams give significance and illumination to our waking consciousness?

A: As far as ordinary dreams are concerned, generally speaking they are seen as an example of something unreal. So, I don't think there is any need to take them too seriously. Of course, there have been thinkers such as Jung and Freud who have taken dreams very seriously.

However, one cannot totally dismiss one's dreams. It is possible that in some cases, due to the aggregation of many factors, there could be significant indications in dreams; some dreams can have great significance. Therefore, one cannot dismiss all dreams.

As for the details or specific techniques of enabling one to have significant dreams, these can be found in the practices of tantra, particularly in Highest Yoga Tantra. However, the reason there is this emphasis on dream yoga practice, the practice associated with dreams in Highest Yoga Tantra, is because the application of certain techniques in dream states can have significant impact on one's practices during the waking state. That's the main reason. Another reason is that when you are in the dream state, it allows you the opportunity, if you can use the techniques properly, to be able to separate your subtle body from the gross levels of corporal existence.

Q: Since anger and other negative emotions arise from causes and conditions and are not generated under our direct control, how is it that we can directly generate intentions to practice loving-kindness and other positive states?

A: An analogy to this point is that ignorance is quite natural. As we grow up, we are quite ignorant. Then with education and learning we acquire knowledge and dispel ignorance. On the other hand if we leave ourselves in an ignorant state without consciously developing our learning, we won't be able to dispel ignorance. In this case, when we talk about ignorance we are not talking about it in the technical Buddhist sense, but rather as a state of lack of knowledge. So if we continue in a natural state without making an effort to dispel it, then its opposing factors or forces do not come naturally.

Similarly, in the case of anger and hatred, although they arise naturally, in order to dispel or overcome them we have to make a conscious decision and deliberately cultivate their antidotes such as love and compassion. Because we gain from this endeavor we should engage in it.

In Buddhist terminology, nirvana, i.e., liberation or freedom, is often described as "the other side" or "the beyond" and our unenlightened state of samsara as "here and now." There is also a sense that unenlightened individuals can only see their immediate surroundings; they can only see what is obvious. Similarly, what is implied is that many of the negative tendencies, delusory states of mind, emotional afflictions, thoughts, and so on, which are the causes of our own suffering, exist in samsara and they in some sense belong to "this side," so they come quite naturally. On the other hand, most of the positive qualities that need to be generated belong to "the other side," "the beyond," the side of liberation and freedom and nirvana. So unless we consciously develop them, these qualities will not arise naturally.

If we are successful in "going beyond," we can adopt a perspective from which many of the negative tendencies, the delusory states of mind, and so forth, become the "other side."

Q: If hatred comes in part from a sense of having been wronged or being hurt, is it not less evil, less negative, than doing harm coldly? Or is there always hatred beneath the harm, as with the harm that has been done to the Tibetan people?

A: That is quite a complicated question.

The first part is a very complicated question, and I think one has to distinguish between many different situations.

Some harms can be inflicted without any sense of particular hatred, but out of ignorance. For instance, we eat a lot of fish. And when we fish, there is no feeling of a fish being a sentient or living being. But there is no hatred. The killing is done out of ignorance.

Then there is another kind of killing, such as hunting for pleasure. Again, there is no hatred. I think this is also mainly due to ignorance, and perhaps it also involves greed. In addition, there are cases in which killing or hunting are mainly a question of survival. So there are a lot of differences.

Then, I think the Nazis' extermination of the Jews and other people in the concentration camps is yet another case. It is possible that even in such extreme cases there may be a few individuals involved who do not have a personal feeling of hatred. Because of this complexity, and the complex nature of human actions, in the

Buddhist doctrine of karma we make distinctions between four principal categories of action: actions which, though committed, are in some sense motiveless; actions which have been committed only in motivation, but are not fully executed; actions which have both full completion of the motivation and execution; and those which are neither motivated nor executed. There is also such a thing as "mercy killing." So between ignorance-motivated killing and hatred-motivated killing, I would think that killing motivated by hatred is graver and more negative.

Even for a given action, an act of killing, for instance, there may be different degrees of negative karma accumulated by the person depending on various factors that are complete or incomplete. For instance, you can have an individual act of killing where a person has a very strong desire to kill, a very strong negative emotion, and even the method of killing is very cruel. If the killing is motivated out of hatred, then, of course, the methods would be very cruel. Then at the conclusion of the act, the killer could have some sense of satisfaction of having accomplished it. In such a case, the negative karma that is accumulated is considered to be the gravest. However, there are cases where there is less strong emotion at the time of the motivation and the methods which are used for killing are less cruel, and the person may feel regret at the time that the killing is done. Under such circumstances, the negative karma accumulated is considered to be comparatively less.

In addition, within the type of killing which is committed through hatred, there can be various degrees of hatred. Hatred can be very subtle. Further, if the murder is planned for many years, when it takes place, there is no anger. But you can't say that in such cases there is no hatred. There is hatred deep down. Yet at the very instant when the action is committed, there is no strong emotion.

There is a Tibetan saying that the more sophisticated a person is, the more skillful the person may be in hiding his or her feeling of hatred. So the angrier a person is, or the more hateful a person is, the gentler the person will appear. I don't know whether that is to be valued or not.

Q: Would you speak more on the purpose of life, please. It sounds frivolous for the purpose of life to be joy and happiness. So much needs to be done, and it all seems far from easy and happy. It seems selfish to be happy when so many sad things are going on.

A: I believe the purpose of life is happiness. So what is happiness? There are many levels. The highest happiness is Buddhahood; the state of Buddhahood is the most profoundly happy state. The next happiest state is nirvana, being an Arhat in nirvana. Of course, that state does not give one total satisfaction as there are still some defects in the mind, but there is no longer any suffering due to ignorance, so it is also one happy state of mind. Then thinking about the next life and a good birth is also defined as happiness. But in lower realms, there is more suffering and because of that, a rebirth into a lower realm is not desirable. We are trying to get to the higher birth. Why? There is more happiness.

But then, within this life, I think the very existence of day-to-day life is very much alive with hope, although there is no guarantee of one's future. There is no guarantee that tomorrow at this time we will all be here. Still, we are working for that purely on the basis of hope. Therefore, for these reasons, I believe life is happiness; this is my belief. This is not necessarily a selfish feeling. It is for serving others, and certainly not for creating misery for them. Serving means not only to enjoy happiness oneself, but also to help other people, other sentient beings, have more happiness. I think that is the whole philosophy, the whole basis. So happiness is not a simple thing.

Q: Please elaborate on how intelligence is a complementary factor for patience.

A: When we go through many of the techniques that are outlined in the text, we have to use a lot of reasoning or analysis. This is what is meant by intelligence being a complementary factor. So at a high level the insight of wisdom can be of many different types. At a higher spiritual level the complementary factor of wisdom could be that of insight into the dynamic, momentarily changing nature of phenomena, or insight into the ultimate nature of reality, and so on. These could serve as complementary factors to one's practice of patience.

Q: What is the Buddhist position on abortion?

A: Regarding birth control in general Buddhists believe that human life is something precious, even though there are a lot of people who are troublemakers! So, as far as controlling this precious life is concerned, it is not advisable. However, today there are too many precious lives—more than five billion. This is the reality. There is also another dimension to the question. The global economic gap between the "northerners" and the "southerners" is not only morally wrong, but practically wrong as well. If it continues it can be a source of problems. Because of the economic gap, many refugees are coming to industrialized nations. That also creates a lot of problems, particularly in Europe. In America there may be fewer problems because it is a vast land, although there is a lot of crime. Therefore, we have to make every effort to reduce this gap. Then, according to specialists, the natural resources simply do not exist to provide the southerners with the standard of living that the northerners are already enjoying, even with this population of five billion. So the entire human population is now facing a problem. Logically, we have to think very seriously about birth control.

Generally speaking, abortion is negative, for it is an act of killing. The other day I read about the human rights of fetuses. That's very, very true from the Buddhist viewpoint, because the unborn fetus is also considered to be sentient, a living being.

For instance, one of the root precepts or root vows of a fully ordained monk or nun is not to kill another human being. If a fully ordained monk or nun kills an unborn fetus, that constitutes breaking the root vow. But then again, the basic Buddhist way of viewing these things is that the most important thing is to judge according to the circumstances. You may have a generalization, but always there will be exceptional cases, which even include mercy killing. Of course, generally speaking, abortion must be avoided. But under certain unique circumstances abortion may be an understandable option. For example, if the mother's and child's lives are at serious risk. Or if there would be some negative serious consequences to the family.

Similarly, on the question of euthanasia, from the Buddhist viewpoint if keeping a patient alive longer is very expensive, and if it would cause difficulty for the remaining family, and if there is no hope so that the patient will remain in a coma with no mental functioning, then it may be acceptable. Of course if the family has enough money, and if they want to keep the patient alive, it's their right. But if the circumstances are such that it creates a lot of problems, then euthanasia, in such exceptional cases, may be possible. Similarly abortion under particular circumstances may be possible. But we have to judge on the spot, case-by-case. That's the general Buddhist approach.

SECOND SESSION

(34) If things were brought into being by choice,
Then since no one wishes to suffer,
Suffering would not occur
To any embodied creature.

(35) Through not being careful
People even harm themselves with thorns and other things,
And for the sake of obtaining women and the like
They become obsessed and deprive themselves of food.

In verses 34 and 35, Shantideva explains another way to deal with harm or injury by developing a sense of indifference toward the actual perpetrator of the crime or the aggressor. He suggests that in many cases, if one examines the situation carefully one will find that many of these actions are committed either out of ignorance or carelesssness or that there is not much choice on the part of the other person. If this were not the case, why would people also sometimes injure or hurt themselves? So if one examines this situation carefully, one will see that many harmful acts are caused not out of malicious intention, but out of carelessness or a lack of sensitivity.

> (36) And there are some who injure themselves
> Through the unmeritorious deeds
> Of hanging themselves, leaping from cliffs,
> Eating poison and unhealthy food.

> (37) If, when under the influence of disturbing
>   conceptions,
> People will even kill their treasured selves,
> How can they be expected not to cause harm
> To the bodies of other living beings?

In verse 37, Shantideva states that if it is possible for individuals to injure themselves or cause harm to themselves out of ignorance or carelessness, then it is also possible that they would inflict harm on others in the same manner. If they are prepared to inflict harm on themselves, it is very possible that they would inflict harm on others as well.

> (38) Even if I cannot develop compassion for all such people
> Who through the arisal of disturbing conceptions
> Set out to try and kill me and so forth,
> The last thing I should do is to become angry with them.

So in verse 38, he suggests that regarding those people who commit such acts of harm or injury upon themselves and others, instead of feeling hateful or angry toward them, the appropriate attitude that one should develop is compassion.

(39) Even if it were the nature of the childish
To cause harm to other beings,
It would still be incorrect to be angry with them,
For this would be like begrudging fire for having the nature
    to burn.

(40) And even if the fault were temporary
In those who are by nature reliable,
It would still be incorrect to be angry,
For this would be like begrudging space for allowing smoke
    to rise in it.

In the next verses, Shantideva presents ways in which we can prevent the causes that would normally give rise to anger within us. He states that if inflicting harm upon others is in some sense an inalienable part of the nature of a person, then there is no point in holding it against him or her. After all, that person cannot help it. Harming others is that person's essential nature. On the other hand, if it is not his or her essential nature, but rather some sort of circumstantial phenomenon, then when the person is in a fit of anger he or she is under the influence of a circumstantial condition, for which there is no point in holding him or her accountable.

In the former case, it is analogous to begrudging fire because it burns; the ability to burn is part of the essential nature of fire. So to begrudge fire for possessing that nature is quite pointless. In the latter case, if one holds a grudge against sentient beings who are under the influence of a circumstantial condition, then it is quite similar to someone who begrudges clouds that overcast the sky. It is not the essential nature of the sky to be overcast, but through circumstantial conditions, sometimes the sky is obscured by clouds.

(41) If I become angry with the wielder
Although I am actually harmed by his stick,

Then, since he too is secondary, being in turn incited by
hatred,
I should be angry with his hatred instead.

In verse 41, Shantideva points out another method through
which one can attempt to prevent the arisal of anger or defuse the
force of anger: by examining both the immediate and long-term factors which gave rise to the particular act or injury. On the one hand,
we could say that it is the factor that directly causes the pain that
one should feel angry toward. If, for instance, someone hits one with
a stick, then it is in fact the stick toward which one should direct
one's anger. On the other hand, we could say that it is the root or
underlying cause that gives rise to the act with which one should feel
angry. In this case, since it is hatred which is the motivating factor
of the act, one should direct one's anger toward that hatred. So why
is it that we particularly select the intermediary between the direct
cause of our injury, which is the stick, and the indirect, underlying
cause, the hatred? We leave these two aside and particularly select
the intermediary, the person, and direct all our anger against the
person. Shantideva questions the whole rationale behind this.

(42) Previously I must have caused similar harm
    To other sentient beings.
    Therefore it is right for this harm to be returned
    To me who is the cause of injury to others.

Then in verse 42, he discusses the possibility of another consideration or reflection on the same act, which is the act of injury
caused by someone hitting us with a stick. He points out that since
all our painful experiences are consequences of our own negative
deeds committed in the past, if one were to hold responsible all
of the factors that gave rise to that injury, then one should also
include oneself because after all it is due to one's own karmic deeds
that one is suffering that particular injury or harm.

(43) Both the weapon and my body
Are the causes of my suffering.
Since he gave rise to the weapon and I to the body,
With whom should I be angry?

In verse 43, Shantideva observes that it is through a combination of various factors and conditions that we experience pain. For instance, in the case of someone hitting us with a weapon, the contributing factors are the weapon which is wielded by the other person and also our own body, because the very nature of the body is that it has a capacity for feeling the pain of injury. Without the body as a basis, an experience of pain or injury could not arise in the first place. So, since both the other's weapon and my own body in combination give rise to this injury and harm, why do I particularly single out that other factor as the object of my anger?

For example, if you know that someone is speaking badly of you behind your back, and if you react to that negativity with a feeling of hurt or anger, then you yourself destroy your own peace of mind. One's pain is one's own creation. There is a Tibetan expression that one should treat such things as if they were wind behind one's ear. In other words, just brush it aside. If one were to do that, one would protect oneself from that feeling of hurt and agony. This shows that to a large extent whether or not one suffers pain depends on how one responds to a given situation. What makes a difference is whether or not one is too sensitive and takes things too seriously.

So from the Buddhist viewpoint, in our daily life we are sometimes too sensitive toward minor things. At the same time, toward other major problems that can create long-term consequences, we are not so sensitive. Because of this, we find in the scriptures that ordinary people like ourselves are described as childlike or childish. In fact, the term *jhipa* (Tib. *byis pa*), or childish, is used in different ways: sometimes it is used in terms of age, which is the conventional usage; sometimes it is used for ordinary sentient beings, as opposed to the Arya beings, the superior beings. Then sometimes it is used to describe people who are concerned only with affairs of this life and have no interest or regard for the affairs of their future life, or life after death. So, the tendency of our childish nature is to take small things too seriously and get easily offended, whereas when we are confronted with situations which have long-term consequences, we tend to take things less seriously.

> (44) If in blind attachment I cling
> To this suffering abscess of a human form
> Which cannot bear to be touched,
> With whom should I be angry when it is hurt?

In verse 44, Shantideva notes that so long as we possess this aggregate, the mind-body composite, which is a product of our karma and delusions, we are always prone to pain, suffering, and dissatisfaction.

> (45) It is the fault of the childish that they are hurt,
> For although they do not wish to suffer
> They are greatly attached to its causes.
> So why should they be angry with others?

> (46) Just like the guardians of the hell worlds
> And the forest of razor-sharp leaves,
> So is this (suffering) produced by my actions;
> With whom therefore should I be angry?

In verse 45, Shantideva states that much of our pain and suffering is caused by this childish nature, which makes us take small things too seriously and remain indifferent to concerns that have long-term implications and consequences. Therefore, since our pain and suffering are, in fact, of our own doing, why should we hold others responsible and accountable for our experience of pain and suffering?

For example, after the Gulf War, many people blamed the conflict on Saddam Hussein. Based on this same concept, on various occasions I said, "That's not fair." Under such circumstances, I really feel sympathy toward Saddam Hussein. Of course, he is a dictator, and of course, there are many other bad things there, but without military equipment an army cannot cause harm. All this equipment was not produced by them. So, when we look at it like that, many nations were involved. But our normal tendency is to try to blame it on another, an external factor. This tendency is to focus on one single cause, and then try to exonerate oneself from responsibility.

So I think this mental practice is to look at it in a holistic way, to see that there are many events involved. We cannot pinpoint responsibility for what happened entirely on one person. As another example, consider our problem with the Chinese. I think many contributions were made from the Tibetan side that led to this tragic situation. Perhaps our generation made some contributions, but definitely the previous generations did, for at least a few generations' time. So it is not fair to blame everything on China.

So if we examine any given situation in an unbiased and honest way, and also from a wide perspective, then we realize that, to a large extent, we are also responsible for the unfolding of events.

> (47) Having been instigated by my own actions,
> Those who cause me harm come into being.
> If by these (actions) they should fall into hell
> Surely isn't it *I* who am destroying them?

In verse 47, Shantideva points out that it is our negative karma and deeds committed in the past that have caused the other person to inflict that injury or harm on us. In addition, because of that negative act, the person creates negative karma. So in a sense, we are causing the downfall of the other person because we are, through our karma, forcing the other person, the perpetrator of the crime or the aggressor, to create negative karma.

> (48) In dependence upon them I purify many evils
> By patiently accepting the harms that they cause.

But in dependence upon me they will fall
Into hellish pain for a very long time.

(49) So since I am causing harm to them
And they are benefitting me,
Why, unruly mind, do you become angry
In such a mistaken manner?

In verses 48 and 49, Shantideva observes that from one point of view, as pointed out earlier, when the other person inflicts harm or injury upon one, that person is accumulating negative karma. However, if one examines this carefully, one will see that because of that very act, one is given the opportunity to practice patience and tolerance. So from our point of view it is an opportune moment, and we should therefore feel grateful toward the person who is giving us this opportunity. Seen in this way, what has happened is that this event has given another an opportunity to accumulate negative karma, but has also given us an opportunity to create positive karma by practicing patience. So why should we respond to this in a totally perverted way, by being angry when someone inflicts harm on us, instead of feeling grateful for the opportunity?

(50) If my mind has the noble quality (of patience)
I shall not go to hell,
But although I am protecting myself (in this way)
How will it be so for them?

At this point, two questions are raised. First, since it is the case that when the other person inflicts harm on me I am giving that person an opportunity to create negative karma, does that mean I will also accumulate negative karma because I am causing the downfall of the other person? Shantideva responds by saying no, because if one takes that opportunity to respond in a positive way, to practice patience and tolerance instead of accumulating negative karma, one will be accumulating virtues or positive karma.

Second, if by inflicting injury upon me the other person has given me this opportunity to practice patience and tolerance, and thereby allows me to accumulate virtuous karma, does that mean that the person who has inflicted the harm also accumulates virtuous karma? Shantideva responds by suggesting that this is not the case because the result, the virtuous karma of practicing patience and tolerance, will be established only in the mind of the person who is practicing patience and tolerance.

(51) Nevertheless, should I return the harm
It will not protect them either.
By doing so my conduct will deteriorate
And hence this fortitude will be destroyed.

Shantideva states that if we respond to harm or injury inflicted upon us by retaliating against the other person, then not only will that act be of no use to the other person—in fact it will be harmful to him or her—it will also be destructive so far as our own interests are concerned. This is because if one is a practitioner of bodhichitta, it will deteriorate one's bodhichitta practice. Additionally, it will weaken the fortitude that one has built through the practice of tolerance and patience. So it is destructive both for the other and for oneself.

When someone inflicts harm or injury upon us, if instead of responding positively by developing patience and tolerance we retaliate and take revenge upon him or her, then it will establish a kind of vicious circle. If one retaliates, the other is not going to accept that and he or she is going to retaliate, and then one will do the same, and it will go on. When this happens at the community level, it can go on from generation to generation in a vicious circle. So the result is that both sides suffer. The whole purpose of life is spoiled. For example, in the refugee camps, from childhood hate grows, and some people consider that strong hatred good for the national interest. I think this is very negative, very short-sighted.

In our discussion earlier, we talked about how to respond

appropriately to physical injury and harm inflicted by others, and how one should develop tolerance toward them. However, it is important not to misunderstand and think that Shantideva is saying that we should give in, or that we should just meekly accept whatever is done against us.

This is relevant to one of the aspects of Buddhist practice that deals with generosity and giving. We know that according to the Bodhisattva ideal, one's generosity should be so developed that eventually, even if the situation requires the Bodhisattva to sacrifice his or her own body, that Bodhisattva will be able to do so. However, in this regard, a sensitivity to the time factor is crucial. One should not do such practices prematurely, before one has developed the appropriate strength, realization, and so forth, at which one can practice in these ways. So, sensitivity to the appropriateness of time is very important. This is related to what I pointed out earlier: that for a minor purpose, one should not give away or sacrifice something which has higher potential. If this is the case, then of course Shantideva cannot recommend to practitioners of bodhichitta that any harm others inflict, physical injury and so forth, should be meekly accepted. Rather, if necessary, the best and wisest course might be to simply run away, run miles away!

The reason I state that it is important to be sensitive to the appropriateness of time, depending on the level of one's realization, is because we find in the scriptures stories of great meditators who have made such sacrifices. For example, in one of the lives of the Buddha in the *Jataka* tales, he willingly accepts all of the physical injury that is done to him by subjecting his body to be severed, cut, mutilated, and so on. He did not avoid such situations but, rather, faced them. This type of practice can be undertaken by individuals who have reached higher levels of realization and know that by doing so they might achieve a great purpose.

What all these examples point out is that it is essential, when one engages in practice, to be able to weigh the circumstances, the long-term and short-term consequences, and the pros and cons of the situation.

Generally speaking, Vinaya, which is the category of scripture that deals with ethics and monastic discipline, tends to be less flexible on ethical questions than the Mahayana stance. Even there, Buddha taught about various acts which would be universally proscribed or prohibited, and then pointed out exceptional cases, under new circumstances, in which the same act could be permitted. Similarly, he taught various universal affirmative precepts that his disciples must follow. Then, under certain circumstances, he would give exceptions for certain individuals or for specific times when there was no need to adhere to the precept. So, even from the Vinaya standpoint, where there is less flexibility on these issues, we again find a sensitivity to context and situation.

We have been discussing injury and harm mainly in terms of physical injury and physical harm inflicted by others upon oneself, how to deal with them, and how to respond appropriately toward such an act. In the next verses, Shantideva talks about how to deal with types of injury which are not physical, such as feelings of hurt caused by someone insulting or belittling us.

> (52) Since my mind is not physical
> In no way can anyone destroy it,
> But through its being greatly attached to my body
> It is caused harm by (physical) suffering.

> (53) Since disrespect, harsh speech
> And unpleasant words
> Do not cause any harm to my body,
> Why mind, do you become so angry?

In verses 52 and 53, Shantideva reminds us that mind is not physical and talks about the relationship between the body and the mind. And he asks, in the case of someone being disrespectful or using harsh speech and insulting us and so on, since that person does not cause any direct physical injury, why should the mind be angry toward him or her?

(54) —Because others will dislike me—
But since it will not devour me
Either in this life or in another life
Why do I not want this (dislike)?

Here Shantideva anticipates the defense that although it is correct that insults and disrespect and so on do not cause any direct physical injury or harm, these will lead others to dislike me; therefore, I must feel angry toward them. Shantideva argues that this is not an adequate ground on which to feel angry toward such acts, because even if others dislike me it is not going to cause any serious downfall to me in this lifetime or in a future lifetime. On the contrary, if one responds to these acts by others in a negative way, by losing one's temper and being angry, then the end result is that one will lose oneself, because this response will destroy one's peace and calmness of mind. It is we who stand to lose.

So here again Shantideva is not suggesting that we should act in a way that totally disregards the opinions of others, or that we shouldn't care about what other people think. One should not misunderstand Shantideva as recommending that we act in that way. On the contrary, we find in the *Guide to the Bodhisattva's Way of Life* itself one verse in which Shantideva states that whenever one moves into a new area or town, one should learn the ways of the particular community, learn to live in a way which will not offend the other people. This is because if one can make others happy, then one will be in a better position to be of service to them. That is one principle of a Bodhisattva. So one should not misunderstand here, thinking that Shantideva is suggesting that we should be totally negligent of others. What is being said is contextualized; that is, in order to prevent the arising of anger toward another's insult or disrespect, and so forth, one should think in this manner. But this is a very specific context.

(55) —Because it will hinder my worldly gain—
Even if I do not want this

I shall have to leave my worldly gains behind
And my evil alone will remain unmoved.

In this verse, Shantideva anticipates another defense, the argument that we might feel justified in retaliating against someone insulting us, speaking badly of us, or belittling us, because these activities will hinder our worldly gains, successes, and achievements: if we don't retaliate against such acts, then they will obstruct our worldly achievements. Shantideva says that this is not an adequate ground upon which to retaliate against others' insults or belittling acts. After all, even if such acts of others do hinder our worldly gain, worldly gains are ultimately to be left behind. They are of benefit and use only in this lifetime, but when one dies one has to leave them behind, so they are not of that much importance. By responding negatively to others' insults or belittling acts, for instance if one loses one's temper and acts in a negative way, then the negative karma which has been created by these acts is something that one has to carry along with one, even into future lives.

(56) Thus it is better that I die today
Than live a long but wicked life;
For even if people like me should live a long time,
There will always be the suffering of death.

(57) Suppose someone should awaken from a dream
In which he experienced one hundred years of happiness,
And suppose another should awaken from a dream
In which he experienced just one moment of happiness;

(58) For both of these people who have awoken
That happiness will never return.
Similarly, whether my life has been long or short,
At the time of death it will be finished like this.

(59) Although I may live happily for a long time
Through obtaining a great deal of material wealth,
I shall go forth empty-handed and destitute
Just like having been robbed by a thief.

In these verses, Shantideva points out that compared to someone living a long life based on material successes which are acquired
through wrong means of livelihood, it is better to die today, because
sooner or later one will die and the things that one has acquired
will be left behind. However, the negative fruits of the wicked
actions that one has committed will be carried over long into the
future. In any case, the temporary pleasure or happiness that one
might gain from living a materially successful life through wicked
means or wrong livelihood, at the time of death, no matter how
long one has lived that way, it becomes only an insignificant object
of memory, something like a past dream. There is no qualitative
difference between that and someone living a happy sort of life in
a single instant: once they are past, they are just like dreams.

(60) —Surely material wealth will enable me to live,
And then I shall be able to consume evil and do good—
But if I am angry on account of it
Will not my merit be consumed and evil increase?

(61) And what use will be the life
Of one who only commits evil,
If for the sake of material gain
He causes (the merits needed for) life to degenerate?

Here Shantideva anticipates another response by stating that
someone might feel, "Surely through acquiring material wealth
I will not only live more comfortably but will also gain the opportunity to do a lot of wholesome deeds and earn merit from it.
Because of this fact, surely I am justified in retaliating against

any act committed by another that comes in the way of acquiring this wealth." Shantideva says that this again is not an adequate ground for behaving in this way because when one compares the opportunity for accumulating merit by engaging in wholesome actions that is obtained through acquiring material wealth to the negative karma one creates by retaliating against another person who insults one and so forth, there is simply no comparison: the negative actions far outweigh the few wholesome deeds one might engage in. Therefore, it cannot justify retaliation against someone who insults or belittles one.

> (62) —Surely I should be angry with those
> Who say unpleasant things that weaken other beings'
>   (confidence in me)—
> But in the same way why am I not angry
> With people who say unpleasant things about others?

> (63) If I can patiently accept this lack of confidence
> Because it is related to someone else,
> Then why am I not patient with unpleasant words (about
>   myself)
> Since they are related to the arisal of disturbing
>   conceptions?

Here, Shantideva anticipates another defense by stating that someone could say, "Surely when someone insults me, or is being disrespectful, or speaks badly of me, I am justified in feeling angry toward that person because this will cause others to lose confidence in me."

Shantideva argues that if this is truly justified, if this is the case, then why should one not be angry toward other people speaking badly of a third person? Then, one might respond to this by saying, "Come on here, when someone is insulting a third person, it has nothing to do with me."

Meditation

For this session, let us do a meditation visualizing someone whom you dislike, someone who annoys you, causes a lot of problems for you, gets on your nerves. Imagine a scenario where the person irritates you, does something that offends or annoys you. And, in your imagination, when you visualize this, let your natural response follow, flow. And then see whether that causes the rate of your heartbeat to go up. See your mental feelings and whether there is an immediately uncomfortable feeling, or if you develop even more peace. Judge and investigate for three or four minutes. Then, for the last minute, understand that it is of no use if we let the irritation develop: immediately we lose our peace of mind. So say to yourself, "In the future, I will never do this." Develop the determination and then relax in absorptive meditation.

Questions

Q: Besides contemplating one's suffering, are there any other techniques or antidotes to cultivate in order to work with pride?

A: One antidote is to reflect upon the diversity of disciplines. According to Buddhism, one of the antidotes of pride is to reflect upon the multiple categories one finds in the sutras, the various ways in which one can perceive reality, and so on. Another example is the modern educational system, in which there are multiple disciplines. Thinking about the many fields of knowledge in which one is ignorant can help overcome pride.

Q: What role does forgiveness have in enhancing tolerance and patience?

A: Forgiveness is something like an end result, or a product, of patience or tolerance. When one is truly patient and tolerant, then forgiveness comes naturally. So they are very intimately connected.

Q: What is the position of women in Buddhism? We have all heard of the excesses, prejudices, and outright misconduct with which women are treated in Buddhism as well as in other religions. But Buddhist texts seem to speak to a male point of view. Women seem to have a different set of social and physical issues. Are there different practices, texts, etc., for laywomen and nuns to assist us through the denser aspects of the path? How does a nun's life differ from a monk's?

A: It is very true that because many of the Indian pundits whom we cite as authorities, as sources for Buddhist literature and thought in Tibet, were male practitioners, so often their writings reflect principally a male point of view.

The second point you raised is a little bit more complicated. First, according to Vinaya rules, Buddha gave equal opportunities to males and females. In the *Vinaya Sutra*, there is provision for full ordination of both men and women. However, I think because of cultural aspects the *bhikshu* is considered higher and the *bhikshuni* next. So from that angle, there is an element of discrimination.

Similarly in all practices of the Bodhisattva and tantric vows, both male and female practitioners are equal. There are, however, certain texts where we find statements to the effect that a Bodhisattva who is in the final stage of attending full enlightenment is necessarily in a male form.

According to the perspective of Highest Yoga Tantra, not only are there equal opportunities on the path, but also any practitioner can attain full enlightenment, in either the male or the female form. So there is no distinction or discrimination there. However, it seems very clear that in the Highest Yoga Tantra, special attention is paid to the rights of women, because when listing the tantric vows in Highest Yoga Tantra, not abusing or insulting women is counted as one of the root vows. The reason for listing those, I think, is because at the societal level there is some prejudice against women. So, particular attention is paid to respecting a woman's dignity and rights. In fact, an ideal practitioner of Highest Yoga Tantra is supposed to relate to women in a special way. For a practitioner of the Mother Tantras, there is a special emphasis: if there is no particular objection, then whenever one meets a woman, it is suggested that one prostrate and pay homage. If one cannot physically do that, one is supposed to pay homage mentally.

On the other hand, not abusing a male practitioner or insulting a man is not counted as one of the root vows. What this indicates is that special attention is paid according to the respect that is due. So I think basically equal opportunity is there. However, because of the social system, there is the danger of abuse or looking down on a female. So a special emphasis is placed that I think clearly elucidates complete equality. If one looks at it from the whole Bodhisattva approach, I think it is quite equal.

The Goddess Tara, I think, is one of the most influential feminists. The legend of Tara shows that when she first generated the altruistic intention to become fully enlightened for the benefit of others, she made a resolution. Seeing that there were so many Bodhisattvas who were male, and so many Bodhisattvas on the path were male, and so many who had attained Buddhahood in the male form, she was determined not only to generate bodhichitta in her present form as a female, but also to retain the same female form while on the path, and also to retain it when she became fully enlightened.

Q: Can you discuss the problem of self-hatred, and the Buddhist means to alleviate it?

A: In fact, when I first heard the word "self-hatred" and was first exposed to the concept of self-hatred, I was quite surprised and taken aback. The reason why I found it quite unbelievable is that as practicing Buddhists, we are working very hard to overcome our self-centered attitude, and selfish thoughts and motives. So to think of the possibility of someone hating themselves, not cherishing oneself, was quite unbelievable. From the Buddhist point of view, self-hatred is very dangerous because even to be in a discouraged state of mind or depressed is seen as a kind of extreme. Because self-hatred is far more extreme than being in a depressed state, it is very, very dangerous.

So the antidote is seen in our natural Buddha-nature—the acceptance or belief that every sentient being, particularly a human being, has Buddha-nature. There is a potential to become a Buddha. In fact, Shantideva emphasizes this point a great deal in the *Guide to the Bodhisattva's Way of Life*, where he states that even such weak sentient beings as flies, bees, and insects possess Buddha-nature, and if they take the initiative and engage in the path, they have the capacity to become fully enlightened. If that is the case, then why not I, who am a human being and possess human intelligence and all the faculties, if I make the initiative, why can't I also become fully enlightened? So this point is emphasized. In his text called *Sublime Continuum*, Maitreya presents the Buddhist view on the doctrine of Buddha-nature. It states that no matter how poor or weak or deprived one's present situation may be, a sentient being never loses his or her Buddha-nature. The seed, the potential for perfection and full enlightenment, always remains.

For people who have the problem of self-hatred or self-loathing, for the time being it is advisable that they not think seriously about the suffering nature of existence or the underlying unsatisfactory nature of existence. Rather they should concentrate more on the positive aspects of existence, such as appreciating the potentials that lie within oneself as a human being, the opportunities that one's existence as a human being affords. In the traditional teaching, one speaks about all the qualities of a fully endowed human existence. By reflecting upon these opportunities and potentials, one will be able to increase one's sense of worth and confidence.

So what is important here is, again, a very skillful approach, an approach that is most suited and appropriate to one's own mental faculties, disposition, and interests. As an analogy, suppose one needs to get another person from one town to another quite far away, and suppose that person is not very courageous. If one tells him or her about the difficulties, then the person may feel totally discouraged and disheartened or lose hope and think, "Oh, I'll never get there." However, one can achieve the purpose through more skillful means, leading that person step by step, first by saying, "Oh, let us go to this town," and then once there, saying, "Oh, let's go to the other town." This is also analogous to our educational system. Although our aim may be to go to the university and get a higher education, we cannot start right from there. We have to begin at the primary level, where we start with the alphabet and so on. As one progresses, then one will go to the next stage, and the next, and so on. In this way, one will be able to reach the ultimate aim. Similarly, in the case of Dharma practice, it is very important to adopt the methods most suited to one's current condition. For instance, different people have different temperaments: some people may be more arrogant and conceited, and they should adopt a path or a method which is more suited to that type of temperament. Some people may have stronger desire or anger, or whatever it may be; then that type of person may have to look for a technique or method which is more suited to that tendency. And some people may have less courage and confidence in themselves, and such a person needs to engage in an approach which is more suited to that type of temperament. So we find that in Āryadeva's text called *Four Hundred Verses*, he talks quite extensively about how best to lead a student along the path, according to each mental disposition.

In fact, there is a historical precedent here. In Buddha's time there was a king who committed the heinous crime of murdering his father. But he was totally overwhelmed by his crime, and depressed. When Buddha visited him he made a statement and said that parents are to be killed, but he didn't mean it literally. Buddha was using parents as a kind of metaphor for desire and attachment that lead to rebirth. Because karma and desire combine to create rebirth, in some sense they are like parents. So in making that statement that parents are to be killed, he meant that karma and desire are to be eliminated.

It is from the point of view of the importance of being sensitive to the needs of individual practitioners that one should understand

Buddha's pronouncements in some of the sutras in which he seems to accept even the theory of a self, or soul.

Q: Recognizing the nature of samsara will lead one to develop genuine renunciation. How does one recognize the nature of samsara? Is it the amount of suffering that causes one to develop renunciation, or is it recognizing the nature of suffering that causes one to develop renunciation?

A: Recognition of suffering alone does not guarantee that you will generate genuine renunciation. What is required, in addition, is the recognition of the origin of suffering, and how it leads to suffering. Through the combination of these two, realizing suffering and recognizing the origin of suffering, one will be led to renunciation.

It is stated that among the three types of sufferings—obvious suffering, the suffering of change, and the suffering of pervasive conditioning—the wish to get rid of obvious suffering is something that even animals have instinctively. That cannot be said to be renunciation. One can say that it tends toward renunciation in that it seeks freedom from suffering, but one cannot say it is genuine renunciation.

Seeing the suffering of change as the nature of suffering and developing the wish to be free from it is something which even non-Buddhist meditators, whose primary concern is to seek an absorbed meditative state of mind, can develop. However, this is not the meaning of true renunciation as understood in the Buddhist context. True renunciation has to be developed in relation to the third level of suffering, in which one realizes the underlying, unsatisfactory nature of existence, known as the suffering of pervasive conditioning. When one develops that recognition, one is in fact getting at the root because this recognition is based on the appreciation that one's existence is a product of karma and delusions.

So, as I pointed out earlier, true renunciation must arise as a result of appreciating the dynamic, transient nature of our existence. The momentarily changing nature of phenomena indicates to us our lack of ability to endure, the lack of self-empowerment, the lack of independent status. These things are under the influence of other factors. In the case of our aggregates, the factors that govern them are our karma and delusions, and it is the realization of the negativeness of these causes giving rise to our aggregates that reveals their true unsatisfactory and suffering nature. This will lead to a genuine desire to seek freedom from this particular type of existence. That is true renunciation. Even here, I think that what is necessary in order to develop genuine renunciation is for the individual to have some appreciation of the possibility of freedom, in other words the possibility of attaining nirvana or liberation. Otherwise, if one could develop true renunciation by reflection on the nature of suffering alone, there would have been no need for Buddha to talk about the Four Noble Truths.

He could have simply done away with talking about them. However, when we speak of recognizing the nature of suffering, we have to bear in mind that one can understand its nature in two ways. One is from the ultimate perspective, where we are talking about emptiness, which is the ultimate nature of the reality of suffering. But this is not the understanding we speak of when we discuss the nature of suffering in the context of generating renunciation. Here, we are using more conventional terms.

Q: If the goal is to get rid of emotions, or be free of emotions, how can we feel compassion? Isn't compassion an emotion?

A: You might be interested in hearing about a discussion I had with some scientists. We were talking about how one would define emotion. In the end we all agreed that even at the stage of Buddhahood, we can say that there are emotions. So from that point of view, one could definitely say that compassion is also an emotion.

Emotion is not necessarily something negative. Within emotion, there is both destructive emotion and constructive emotion. So what we should do is eliminate the destructive emotion.

Q: Is it possible for a professed Christian to also take a Buddhist vow? I am a very committed Christian, indeed an ordained person, and yet there seems a compatibility and congruence in my understanding of the teaching of Jesus and that of the Buddhist path of spirituality which would allow assent to both, and practice of both Buddhism and Christianity, as they are pointed toward light, the path of truth, love, and freedom. One of the teachers in my life has been Thomas Merton, a Catholic priest and monk, and a practitioner of Buddhism.

A: Of course, there are many common elements among all major world religious traditions. Therefore, I believe, at the initial stage one person can practice both Buddhism and Christianity simultaneously, and perhaps some other religions as well. I think this is very good.

But the question is when one reaches further. Then it is like in the field of education: when one becomes a specialist, then one has to choose one particular field. In the further practice of Buddhism, when one reaches a certain stage, the realization of emptiness is one of the key aspects of the path. The concept of emptiness and the concept of an absolute Creator, I think, are difficult to put together. On the other hand, for the Christian practitioner, the Creator and the acceptance of the Creator as almighty, is a very important factor within that tradition in order to develop self-discipline, compassion, or forgiveness and to increase them in one's intimate relationship with God. That's something very essential. In addition, when God is seen as absolute and almighty, the concept that everything is relative becomes a little bit difficult. However, if one's understanding of God is in terms of an ultimate nature of reality or ultimate truth, then it is possible to have a kind of unified approach. Then if we try to make a new interpretation, the concept of Father, Son and Holy Ghost, I think might be compared to the *sambhogakaya*, *nirmanakaya*, and *dharmakaya*, the three *kayas*. However, once one begins to interpret the Trinity in terms such as the three-kaya doctrine, then whether that practice truly remains Christian becomes quite questionable.

As to one's personal religion, I think this must be based on one's own mental disposition. That is very important. So I tell people that as a Buddhist monk I find Buddhism is most suitable to me. This does not mean Buddhism is best for everyone. That is clear. For other people, the Christian, Muslim, or Jewish tradition, a tradition which is based on Creator theory, is more effective, that's certain. So it is very, very important to follow religion according to one's own mental disposition.

Then another thing I am always trying to make clear is that changing religion is not a simple task. For example, here in the West, for most of you, your family background and your traditional background are Christian. So I want to warn you that changing religion is very complicated and difficult. Of course, for those individuals who are truly atheists, it doesn't matter if you have more attraction toward Buddhism. Then, good, you should take Buddhism as your religion; that is better than remaining an atheist. Usually I call these people "extreme atheists" because from a certain viewpoint Buddhism is also a kind of atheism. I think it's better than remaining an extreme atheist. So that is clear. But then, for those people who have some religious feeling according to your own tradition, then you must be very careful when considering changing. Generally speaking, I think it is better to practice according to your own traditional background, and certainly you can use some of the Buddhist techniques. Without accepting rebirth theory or the complicated philosophy, simply use certain techniques to increase your power of patience and compassion, forgiveness, things like that.

Also, I think one important thing is single-pointedness meditation, in which there is interest among our Christian brothers and sisters. I have found that in the Greek Orthodox Church it is called "mysticism." So there are, of course, things you can adopt. But otherwise, if you hurriedly change your religion, then after some time you may find some difficulties and some confusion. Therefore, be very careful. An important thing to remember is that once you change your personal religion, there is a natural tendency, in order to justify your newly adopted religion, to take a critical view toward your previous religion. This is very dangerous. Although your previous religion may be unsuitable or ineffective for you, at the same time, millions of people may still get benefit from that tradition. So we must respect each other's individual rights. If it is their belief, and millions of people get their inspiration from it, we must respect that. And there are many reasons to do so.

DAY THREE

FIRST SESSION

Next, Shantideva explains how we should deal with anger and hatred that might arise in us in relation to someone who is destroying something that belongs to us. Up to this point, he has dealt with harm and injury inflicted on oneself; from this point onward, he discusses how to deal with harm inflicted on something that is "mine."

> (64) Should others talk badly of or even destroy
> Holy images, reliquaries and the sacred Dharma,
> It is improper for me to resent it
> For the Buddhas can never be injured.

In verse 64, Shantideva talks about how a Buddhist might try to justify being angry and hateful toward someone who is destroying images of the Buddha or performing sacrilegious deeds such as destroying reliquaries or sacred images, and so forth. For a Buddhist, these are very dear to the heart, very precious. One might try to justify developing hatred toward someone who desecrates these objects by saying that it is for the sake of the Dharma. Shantideva says that this is not the appropriate response, because in reality what is happening is that one is responding because one cannot bear it. But so far as the sacred objects themselves are concerned, they cannot be harmed.

> (65) I should prevent anger arising toward those
> Who injure my spiritual masters, relatives, and friends,

Instead I should see, as in the manner shown before,
That such things arise from conditions.

Then in verse 65, Shantideva says that developing hatred toward
someone who hurts one's spiritual masters, relatives, or friends also
is not appropriate. This is because, even in these cases, the harm
inflicted on these people happens partly because of the karmic
deeds they have performed in the past. On top of that, in some
cases there are also circumstantial conditions involved. If someone is harming one's friend, it may have something to do with the
behavior of that friend—some act of his or hers may have led to the
other person causing him or her harm. So one should take these
factors into account and not feel hatred.

(66) Since embodied creatures are injured
By both animate beings and inanimate objects,
Why only bear malice to the animate?
It follows that I should patiently accept all harm.

In verse 66, Shantideva reflects that since, so far as the factors
that are involved in causing harm and injury are concerned, as
pointed out earlier, there are both animate and inanimate objects.
However, why is it that we specifically single out animate objects
and hold them accountable or bear malice toward them?

(67) Should one person ignorantly do wrong
And another ignorantly become angry (with him)
Who would be at fault?
And who would be without fault?

Here, he shows a symmetry of the two sides. If someone does
harm to one or to one's friends, then that person is doing so principally out of ignorance of the consequences of his or her act. Then
if one were to lose one's temper and be angry toward that person,
again one would be developing anger out of ignorance. So there is

a kind of symmetry between the two acts, and if that is the case, who would be at fault? Who is in the right and who is in the wrong? Both the person who is causing the harm and the person who is being angry are in the same category.

> (68) Why did I previously commit those actions
> Because of which others now cause me harm?
> Since everything is related to my actions
> Why should I bear malice toward these (enemies)?

In this verse, Shantideva responds to a defense one might use which is quite understandable, that someone might try to justify being angry toward another person and saying that these are two different situations: "In the first place, I was just minding my own business. I didn't provoke the other person, and that other person, without any provocation, did this harm to me. So we are not in the same situation. Therefore, my responding with anger is justified."

Shantideva says in this circumstance one hasn't really thought it through enough. If one examines it carefully, one will see that ultimately one is responsible because it is one's own karma that has given rise to this situation. So one cannot say, "I am completely innocent in this situation."

> (69) When I have seen this to be so,
> I should strive for what is meritorious
> (In order to) certainly bring about
> Loving thoughts between all.

In verse 69, Shantideva concludes that by thinking along the lines he has developed earlier, one should resolve, "From now onward I will do my best to ensure that I live in harmony and peace and have loving thoughts when interacting with others. I will do my best not only to ensure that I remain that way, but to ensure that others also do so."

(70) For example, when a fire in one house
Has moved into another house,
It is right to get rid of straw and such things
That will cause the fire to spread.

(71) Likewise when the fire of hatred spreads
To whatever my mind is attached to,
I should immediately get rid of it
For fear of my merit being burned.

In these two verses, Shantideva emphasizes the importance of
dealing with attachment, which is the root, essentially, of hatred
and anger. He gives the example that if one finds one's house is
on fire, then one should try immediately to throwaway all burn-
ing straw in order to ensure that this fire does not spread to other
houses. Similarly, when the fire of hatred spreads then it will spread
because of this fuel of attachment, so what one should be trying to
do is getting rid of attachment. Generally speaking, in Mahayana
literature such as Shantideva's *Compendium of Deeds,* which presents the Bodhisattva ideals or way of life, we find an emphasis
on the importance of dealing with hatred, how to defend oneself
against it and how to eliminate it. However, he mentions that there
are exceptional situations in which attachment could be of assistance to the Bodhisattva who is working for the benefit of others.
Even though this is the case, in general it is attachment or desire
which is at the root of hatred.

The difference between hatred and attachment is that hatred,
when it arises, is very destructive, very rough; it immediately has
an extremely disturbing quality. This is not so much the case with
attachment, which has more gentleness. However, attachment also
is at the root of hatred, so in order to totally eliminate hatred one
must also deal with attachment.

It is important to be clear on this position that although attachment can be of aid or assistance to the Bodhisattva when working
for the benefit of others, this is not due to the nature of attachment,

but rather due to the sophistication of the skillful means which the Bodhisattva can apply in utilizing attachment for the benefit of others. However, one must be clear about the fundamental stand that attachment is at the root of our unenlightened existence.

It is also very clear that many of the conflicts and arguments that one finds, even within the family, are very much based on strong attachment. So we find that there are different types of attachment in relation to different objects: attachment toward form, appearance, sound, smell, tactile sensations, and so on. All of these individually are powerful enough to cause a lot of problems and difficulties. However, the strongest form of attachment seems to be sexual attachment. Where the scripture describes this particular type of attachment, we find attachment toward all the five senses involved. Therefore, it is all the more powerful and has this potential for problems and destruction.

I wonder, however, where the attachment to money belongs, because one cannot say one is attached to the appearance of the form of the money, nor that one is attached to the beautiful sound of it. With money one can acquire a lot of the objects of desire, so maybe it is through that aspect that attachment to money becomes so powerful.

Here it is relevant to discuss intergender relationships. I see two principal types of relationships based on sexual attraction. One form is pure sexual desire in which the motive or impetus is temporary satisfaction, a sort of immediate gratification. Then, based on that, individuals form a relationship, but I think it is not very reliable or stable because the individuals are relating to each other not as people, but rather as objects. However, there is a second type of relationship based on sexual attraction in which the attraction is not predominantly physical. Rather there is an underlying respect and appreciation of the value of the other person, based on one's feeling that the other person is kind, nice, and gentle. One can therefore accord respect and dignity to that other individual. Any relationship which is based on that will be much more long-lasting and also more appropriate. In order to establish that form of relationship, it is crucial for the individuals to have enough time to get to know one another as people. So when each person has enough time to get to know the other at the personal level, to know each other's basic characteristics, then any relationship based on that will be much more reliable and long-lasting. So one could say that in the second type there is some genuine compassion involved in the formation of that relationship. There is a sense of responsibility, because there is a sense of commitment toward each other, whereas in the former case these factors are lacking. There is just temporary satisfaction.

As I mentioned earlier, within oneself, within each single person, one finds many inconsistencies and contradictions. Sometimes the disparity between one's thoughts early and late in the day is so great that one spends all one's energy trying to figure out how it can be resolved. This can lead to headaches. So naturally, between two persons, between parents and children, between brothers and sisters, there are differences. Conflict and disagreements are bound to happen. Given that there are bound to be disagreements, conflicts, contradictions, how do we deal with them, how do we face them? If we have confidence in our capacity for reconciliation then we will be able to deal with these situations.

> (72) Why is a man condemned to death not fortunate
> If he is released after having his hand cut off?
> Why am I who am experiencing human misery not
>   fortunate
> If by that I am spared from (the agonies of) hell?

> (73) If I am unable to endure
> Even the mere sufferings of the present,
> Then why do I not restrain myself from being angry,
> Which will be the source of hellish misery?

In these two verses, Shantideva explains that by not being angry and developing hatred in response to harm caused by others, what one is gaining is protection from potential undesirable consequences that might otherwise come about. Because if one responds to such situations with anger and hatred, not only does it not protect one from the injury that has already been done, but on top of that one creates an additional cause for one's own suffering in the future. However, if one responds without anger and hatred and develops patience and tolerance, then although one may face temporary discomfort or injury, that temporary suffering will protect one from potentially dangerous consequences in the future. If this is the case, then by sacrificing small things, by putting up with small problems or hardships, one will be able to forgo experiences of much greater suffering in the future. An example Shantideva uses here is that if a convicted prisoner can save his life by sacrificing his arm as a punishment, wouldn't that person feel grateful for that opportunity? By accepting the pain and suffering of having his arm cut off, that person will be saving himself from death, which is a greater suffering. Shantideva adds that there is another advantage: not only will one be protected from potentially dangerous consequences in the future, but also by experiencing the pain and suffering which has been caused temporarily by others, one is exhausting the karmic potentials of negative karma which one has accumulated in the past. So it serves two purposes.

Patiently accepting small hardships also gives one the opportunity to apply other practices. One could make aspirational prayers and the dedication, "By my experience of this suffering, may I be able to purify my negativities committed in the past." One can also use the opportunity for the practice of *tong-len*, which is the Mahayana practice of "giving and taking." For that, when one undergoes the experience of pain and suffering one thinks, "May my suffering substitute for all similar types of suffering that sentient beings may have to undergo. May I, by experiencing this, be able to save all other sentient beings from having to undergo the same suffering." So in this way one takes others' suffering upon oneself and uses the experience of hardship as an opportunity for this type of practice as well.

This advice is especially useful when dealing with illnesses. Of course it is important, first of all, to take all the preventative measures so one does not suffer from illnesses, such as adopting the right diet, or whatever it may be. Then when one becomes ill, it is important not to overlook the necessity for taking the appropriate medications and other measures necessary for healing. However, there would be an important difference in how one responded to illness if instead of moaning about the situation, instead of feeling sorry for oneself, instead of being overwhelmed by anxiety and worry, one saved oneself from these unnecessary additional mental pains and suffering by adopting the right attitude. Although it may not succeed in alleviating the real physical pain and suffering, one can think, "May I, by experiencing this pain and suffering, be able to help other people and save others who may have to go through the same experience." One can in this way use that opportunity for a spiritual practice, in other words, practicing *tong-len* meditation, or "giving and taking." This type of practice, although it might not necessarily lead to a real cure in physical terms, can definitely protect one from unnecessary additional mental suffering and pain. And on top of that, it is also possible that instead of being saddened by the experience one can see it as a kind of privilege. One can see it as an opportunity and in fact be joyful because of this particular experience which has made one's life richer.

Sometimes due to misunderstanding the doctrine of karma one has a tendency to blame everything on karma and try to exonerate oneself from responsibility or from the need to take personal initiative. One could quite easily say, "This is due to my negative past karma. What can I do? I am helpless." This is a totally wrong understanding of karma, because although one's experiences are a consequence of one's past deeds, that does not mean that one has no choice, nor that there is no room for initiative to bring about change. This is the same in all areas of life. One should not become passive and try to excuse oneself from having to take personal initiative on the grounds that everything is a result of karma. If we understand the concept of karma properly, we will understand that karma means "action," and it is a very active process.

When we talk of karma or action, it entails action committed by an agent, in this case, oneself, in the past. So what type of future will come about, to a large extent, lies within one's own hands and can be determined by the kind of initiatives that one takes now. Not only that, but karma should not be understood in terms of a passive, static kind of force, but rather in terms of an active process. This indicates that there is an important role for the individual agent to play in determining the course of the karmic process. Consider, for instance, a simple act like fulfilling our need for food. In order to achieve that simple goal one must take action on one's own behalf: one needs to look for food, to prepare it, to eat it. This shows that even a simple act, even a simple goal is achieved through action.

> (74) For the sake of satisfying my desires
> I have suffered numerous burnings in hell,
> But by those actions I fulfilled the purpose
> Of neither myself nor others.

> (75) But now since great meaning will accrue
> From harm which is not even (a fraction) of that,
> I should indeed be solely joyful
> Toward such suffering that dispels the harms of all.

In these verses, Shantideva explains that the hardships, pain, and suffering that one has to undergo in the process of working for the benefit of others, and also in the process of developing patience and tolerance, are almost insignificant when compared to the suffering in lower realms. The forms of suffering which are involved in working for others, through learning or through training, one can definitely put up with.

Meditation

Let us meditate on compassion by visualizing a sentient being who is suffering from acute pain or is in a very unfortunate situation. Then try to relate that being to yourself and think that he or she has the same capacity as you do for experiencing pain, joy, happiness, and suffering. Then simply focus on the unfortunate state of that being's existence, on the intense suffering, and try to develop a natural feeling of compassion toward that sentient being. Let the natural compassion arise in you toward that sentient being.

As before, let us use the first three minutes of the meditation session in a more analytic fashion, thinking about the suffering, its unfortunate state, and so on. Then try to arrive at a conclusion, thinking, "How strongly I wish that sentient being to be free from that suffering," and, "I will help relieve that sentient being from that suffering." Then place your mind single-pointedly on that kind of resolution.

Generally speaking, when we talk about meditation there are two principal types. In one type, you take something as your object of meditation. For example in the case of meditation on impermanence, or meditation on emptiness, you are not generating your mind in the nature of that but rather taking impermanence and emptiness as an object and focusing your mind on that. The other principal type of meditation is one in which you generate your mind into a particular state. For instance, in a meditation on love and compassion you don't take compassion and love as an object of meditation, but rather you try to generate your mind in a loving state or in a compassionate state.

I think it is important to understand that when you develop compassion, by definition you are trying to share the suffering of other sentient beings. From that point of view, you are taking upon yourself additional pain or suffering. There is that element. Because of that, the immediate feeling or sensation within that experience may involve a certain degree of discomfort. However, underlying that, one must have a very high degree of alertness because you are voluntarily and deliberately, for a higher purpose, accepting and taking upon yourself another's suffering. This is very different from the situation in which you think about your own suffering and feel totally overwhelmed by it, where you are burdened by it to the point that your faculties have become numb and dull. The feeling of discomfort that one experiences when taking on others' suffering in generating compassion has an underlying alertness, a sense of deliberation. Therefore, the more suffering you take upon yourself from others, the greater the power of your alertness and determination. So this is a point one has to bear in mind.

One should not misunderstand stories such as that of the great Tibetan Kadampa master Langri Tangpa, who was a great meditator on compassion and love. He was said to be always weeping and in fact was nicknamed "the Weeping Lama." However, this should not be misunderstood, because the very purpose for which that great master found himself weeping all the time was for a state of happiness, total joy, both for others and himself. This state is called *sugata,* which literally means "going to the realm," "going beyond," and is a state of joy and total peace. So Langri Tangpa was not weeping because he wanted to go to a state of suffering, but rather because he wanted to go to, and lead others to, a state of happiness and joy.

QUESTIONS

Q: Please explain the relationships between fear and hatred, and fear and patience.

A: There are many different types of fear. Some fear is genuine, based on valid reasons, and some fear is simply our own mental creation. I think that the second type of fear results from long-term negative consequences and is a state of suffering. Fear of one's own negative emotions, I think, is a valid kind of fear. Fear of others due to one's own negative state of mind can appear to those others as hostility. Due to that, sometimes there is a kind of fear which can be very related to hatred. Fear and patience, I don't know.

Q: Instead of learning to deal with other people's anger, why not simply avoid being with angry people?

A: This is very true. In fact the practitioner, at the initial stage, chooses an isolated place. However this is not a long-term solution; it's a temporary method. While one remains isolated, one must develop inner strength so that when one returns to society, one is already equipped. Someone who totally isolates himself or herself from society and avoids interacting with other people, then spends a whole lifetime in meditation in a solitary retreat, may become an Arhat, which is described as the one who is like a rhinoceros.

Q: What evidence do we have that Buddha-nature exists? How do we know that everyone has this? And that we have it ourselves?

A: First, in Buddhist thought, one of the reasons is that the ultimate nature of mind is its nonsubstantiality, which the Buddhists call emptiness. The apprehension of the intrinsic reality of our mind is thus an illusion, a distorted state of mind which has no grounding in reality, and therefore it can be eliminated and removed. This is a fact which can be understood by inference without relying on scriptural authority. However, this requires not just an intellectual or inferential understanding alone, but must be combined with meditative experience. So through the combination of inferential, intellectual understanding and meditative experience, we can arrive at the knowledge that the ultimate nature of mind is empty, and the delusory states which are rooted in the apprehension of an intrinsic existence of mind can be eliminated.

It is also possible to come quite close to an understanding that the essential nature of mind is pure by focusing one's attention on the fact that when we talk of consciousness, what is characteristic of it is that consciousness is in the nature of mere experience. It is not physical, it is not material, but it is in the nature of mere experience, or luminosity. That fact is something that one can also understand, not necessarily fully but to a large extent, through inference as well. However, the full understanding of the essential nature of mind being pure and being mere luminosity may require one to rely on scriptural authority because it requires being able to distinguish between various levels of mind. These are explained in terms of four different stages of subtle mind culminating in the very subtle consciousness, which is known as the "clear light" nature of mind. It is quite difficult to say that these can be understood fully through reason without relying on scripture.

What is important here is the level of one's own experience in arriving at a certain degree of understanding. One does find in the Vajrayana literature metaphorical reasoning which attempts to establish the existence of what are known as "the eighty conceptions which are indicative of the subtle states of mind," and how they relate to the four stages of the subtle mind. However, I personally feel that it is quite difficult to fully arrive at the conclusion through mere logic and reasoning. We also find in Maitreya's *Sublime Continuum* the argument that the reason we all possess this innate desire to seek happiness and avoid suffering is because it is possible to overcome suffering and attain happiness. There he tries to point toward existence of Buddha-nature.

Q: What do you think about Dharma teachers who speak and write about Dharma beautifully, but do not live it?

A: Because Buddha knew of this potential consequence, he was very strict in prescribing the qualities that are necessary for a person to be qualified as a teacher. Nowadays, it seems, this is a serious issue. First, on the teacher's side: the person who gives some teaching or gives talks on Dharma must have really trained, learned, and studied. Then, since the subject is not history or literature, but rather a spiritual one, the teacher must gain some experience. Then when that person talks about a religious subject with some experience, it carries some weight. Otherwise, it is not so effective. Therefore, the person who begins to talk to others about the Dharma must realize the responsibility, must be prepared. That is very important. Because of this importance, Lama Tsongkhapa, when he describes the qualifications that are necessary for an individual to become a teacher, quotes from Maitreya's *Ornament of Scriptures,* in which Maitreya lists most of the key qualifications that are necessary on the part of the teacher, such as that the teacher must be disciplined, at peace with himself, compassionate, and so on. At the conclusion, Lama Tsongkhapa sums up by stating that those who wish to seek a spiritual teacher must first of all be aware of what the qualifications are that one should look for in a teacher. Then, with that knowledge, seek a teacher. Similarly, those who wish to seek students and become teachers must not only be aware of these conditions, but also judge themselves to see whether they possess these qualities, and if not, work toward possessing them. Therefore, from the teachers' side, they also must realize the great responsibility involved. If some individual, deep down, is really seeking money, then I think it is much better to seek money through other means. So if the deep intention is a different purpose, I think this is very unfortunate. Such an act is actually giving proof to the Communist accusation that religion is an instrument for exploitation. This is very sad.

Buddha himself was aware of this potential for abuse. He therefore categorically stated that one should not live a way of life which is acquired through five wrong means of livelihood. One of them is being deceptive and flattering toward one's benefactor in order to get maximal benefit.

Now, on the students' side, they also have responsibility. First, you should not accept the teacher blindly. This is very important. You see, you can learn Dharma from someone you accept not necessarily as a guru, but rather as a spiritual friend. Consider that person until you know him or her very well, until you gain full confidence and can say, "Now, he or she can be my guru." Until that confidence develops, treat that person as a spiritual friend. Then study and learn from him or her. You also can learn through books, and as time goes by, there are more books available. So I think this is better.

Here I would like to mention a point which I raised as early as thirty years ago about a particular aspect of the guru-disciple relationship. As we have seen with Shantideva's text *Guide to the Bodhisattva's Way of Life*, we find that in a particular context certain lines of thought are very much emphasized, and unless you see the argument in its proper context there is a great potential for misunderstanding. Similarly, in the guru-disciple relationship, because your guru plays such an important role in serving as the source of inspiration, blessing, transmission, and so on, tremendous emphasis is placed on maintaining proper reliance upon and a proper relationship with one's guru. In the texts describing these practices we find a particular expression, which is, "May I be able to develop respect for the guru, devotion to the guru, which would allow me to see his or her every action as pure."

I stated as early as thirty years ago that this is a dangerous concept. There is a tremendous potential for abuse in this idea of trying to see all the behaviors of the guru as pure, of seeing everything the guru does as enlightened. I have stated that this is like a poison. To some Tibetans, that sentence may seem a little bit extreme. However, it seems now, as time goes by, that my warning has become something quite relevant. Anyway, that is my own conviction and attitude, but I base the observation that this is a potentially poisonous idea on Buddha's own words. For instance in the Vinaya teachings, which are the scriptures that outline Buddha's ethics and monastic discipline, where a relationship toward one's guru is very important, Buddha states that although you will have to accord respect to your guru, if the guru happens to give you instructions which contradict the Dharma, then you must reject them.

There are also very explicit statements in the sutras, in which Buddha states that any instructions given by the guru that accord with the general Dharma path should be followed, and any instructions given by the guru that do not accord with the general approach of the Dharma should be discarded.

It is in the practice of Highest Yoga Tantra of Vajrayana Buddhism where the guru-disciple relationship assumes great importance. For instance, in Highest Yoga Tantra we have practices like guru yoga, a whole yoga dedicated toward one's relation to the guru. However, even in Highest Yoga Tantra we find statements which tell us that any instructions given by the guru which do not accord with Dharma cannot be followed. You should explain to the guru the reasons why you can't comply with them, but you should not follow the instructions just because the guru said so. What we find here is that we are not instructed to say, "Okay, whatever you say, I will do it," but rather we are instructed to use our intelligence and judgment and reject instructions which are not in accord with the Dharma.

However, we do find, if we read the history of Buddhism, that there were examples of single-pointed guru devotion by masters such as Tilopa, Naropa, Marpa, and Milarepa which may seem a little extreme. But we find that while these masters, on the surface, may look like outcasts or beggars, or they may have strange behaviors which sometimes lead other people to lose faith, nevertheless when the necessity came for them to reinforce other people's faith in the Dharma and in themselves as spiritual teachers, these masters had a counterbalancing factor—a very high level of spiritual realization. This was so much so that they could display supernatural powers to outweigh whatever excesses people may have found in them, conventionally speaking. However, in the case of some of the modern-day teachers, they have all the excesses in their unethical behaviors but are lacking in this counterbalancing factor, which is the capacity to display supernatural powers. Because of this, it can lead to a lot of problems.

Therefore, as students, you should first watch and investigate thoroughly. Do not consider someone as a teacher or guru until you have certain confidence in the person's integrity. This is very important. Then, second, even after that, if some unhealthy things happen, you have the liberty to reject them. Students should make sure that they don't spoil the guru. This is very important.

Q: With greatest respect, I sit here thinking it is arrogant to state that there is no Creator. Yet I know Buddhism teaches humility. Why do you think that logic can understand the greater whole? Is that simply another form of belief? Finally, what position do intuition and feeling have concerning the statement that there is, or is not, a Creator?

A: So far as the position that there is no Creator is concerned, it seems that there are very explicit references to that in Buddha's own scriptures. For instance, let us take the scripture on dependent origination called *The Rice Sapling Sutra* in which Buddha states that because the cause was produced or generated, the effects followed. We also find references in the works of subsequent Buddhist thinkers such as Shantideva and Chandrakirti. Shantideva is very explicit and very clear about his position on the whole issue of the Creator in the ninth chapter of the *Guide to the Bodhisattva's Way of Life*. Similarly, Chandrakirti is very clear on this position. We also find Dharmakirti, in the second chapter of *Exposition of Valid Means to Cognition*, adopting a very firm and explicit stand on this issue. Dharmakirti discusses a particular verse in which it is stated that the fully enlightened one is the one who has *become* perfected. So this very word, "becoming," is used there to indicate that there is no belief in an eternal or absolute perfected being. Buddha Shakyamuni became fully enlightened through causes, conditions, training, and a process. Hence, the choice of the word "becoming." That is the Buddhist stand.

Then, as I always say, there are five billion human beings and a variety of different dispositions. So in a certain way I think we need five billion religions, because there are such a variety of dispositions. Therefore it should be very clear that for certain people the concept of a Creator is much more beneficial and much more comfortable. So it is much better that those people should follow that tradition. The gist of all of this is that it is important for each individual to embark upon a spiritual path that is most suited to his or her mental disposition, temperament, and belief.

As to the second part of your question, where does this intuition or feeling for the Creator come from? It may have some sociological explanations; the cultural background may also play an important part. The reason I say this is that for many Tibetans, intuition of life after death or rebirth is natural; it's innate and instinctive. So there are no grounds for dispute here.

The most important thing is, if you utilize a religion or different philosophy for argument, I think that's wrong. Just live it. Buddhism is the business of Buddhists; Christianity is the business of Christians. So that is clear. Even in one restaurant, at one table, we eat different dishes and nobody argues. It is the individual's right.

Q: If all of our actions are dependently arising, how can one choose to move toward enlightenment? Does one choose, or is it just the next inevitable step?

A: There is no possibility of progressing to full enlightenment or liberation simply as a result of timely evolution. So if one doesn't take the initiative, and doesn't make the effort on one's part to consciously embark upon a spiritual path to perfection, then it is not possible for an individual to naturally evolve into a more enlightened being.

When talking about emptiness, we find in the scriptures a listing of sixteen different types of emptiness. The emptiness of samsara is called the "emptiness of beginningless and endless." The reason is that if on the part of individuals no initiative is taken and no conscious effort is made, then our existence in the unenlightened state will go on infinitely. However, if a conscious effort is made and initiative is taken, then there is an end to this unenlightenment.

Here I find a great deal of inspiration from a particular concept in the second chapter of Maitreya's *Ornament of Clear Realizations* in which he talks about five characteristics of the Bodhisattva practitioner. He says that so far as the immediate natural inclination is concerned, there may be something definite about it—some people are more inclined toward the individual path to liberation, and some people are more inclined toward the Bodhisattva ideal leading to the Mahayana goal of full Buddhahood. However, from the ultimate point of view, all sentient beings are equal because Buddha-nature pervades all of them. So here we differentiate between the potential possessed by all beings and their ability to realize that potential.

SECOND SESSION

> (76) Should someone else find joyous happiness
> Upon praising (my enemy) as an excellent person,
> Why, mind, do you not praise him too
> And likewise make yourself happy?

Having dealt with how to respond without anger to harm or injury directed both toward oneself and one's relatives and friends, Shantideva now turns to how to deal with the anger that we feel when we hear our so-called enemies being praised by others, or when others speak highly of someone we dislike. Normally we tend to dislike that sort of news, and then we feel angry about it. So Shantideva points out that one shouldn't; that is not the kind of attitude one must adopt. To be angry at hearing other people speaking highly of one's enemies is totally inappropriate, because if one looks at it carefully, one will find that when someone speaks highly of someone one does not like, at least in the mind of the person who is praising this enemy, there is some sense of fulfillment, some satisfaction. That person is doing so because he or she feels joyous and happy about that enemy, and one should rejoice in that because one's enemy has caused that other person to be joyful, happy, and satisfied. So one should rejoice in that, and if possible should also join in the praise rather than trying to obstruct it. That manner of relating to the situation is truly a source of joy. It also will help other people change their attitude toward one as well, because someone who is capable of dealing with that kind of situation in that manner has less of a problem with jealousy, and a person who has less of a problem with jealousy will truly be happier and more pleasant to associate with.

> (77) That joyous happiness of yours
> Would be a source of joy, not something prohibited,
> A precept given by the Excellent Ones
> And a supreme (means) for assembling others.

> (78) It is said that others are made happy through (being praised) in this way.
> But if, in this way, you do not want (them to have) this happiness,
> Then, (since it makes them happy), you should cease giving wages and the like (to your servants).
> But you would be adversely affected both in this and future lives.

Here, Shantideva anticipates another defense by observing that someone might feel, naturally, "I should feel jealous toward an enemy when he or she is being praised by others because that praise will make my enemy happy. Therefore, of course I will be jealous, and of course I will dislike that praise."

Shantideva responds by saying that if that is one's ground for being jealous of, and being angry about that act, then that means that what one dislikes is the existence of joy or happiness in another person. And if that is the case, then why should one work so hard to please other people, doing all sorts of things for others in order to make them feel happy? If one can't bear one's enemy's happiness, then why should one do all sorts of things to make anyone else happy?

> (79) When people describe my own good qualities
> I want others to be happy too,
> But when they describe the good qualities of others
> I do not wish to be happy myself.

(80) Having generated the Awakening Mind
Through wishing all beings to be happy,
Why should I become angry
If they find some happiness themselves?

Shantideva explains in the next verse another inconsistency regarding this issue. He notes that when praise is directed toward oneself, when people speak highly of oneself, one not only feels happy but also expects others to be happy when they hear this praise. However, this is totally inconsistent with one's attitude toward others. When people praise others, then not only does one disapprove of others' happiness but one's own peace of mind and happiness are destroyed as well. So there seems to be an inconsistency when it comes to relating to praise directed toward oneself and praise directed toward others.

Then, especially for a Bodhisattva practitioner who has dedicated his or her life to bringing about joy and happiness in others and leading them to the ultimate state of happiness, to be jealous of others' happiness and joy is totally inappropriate. In fact, one should feel that if other sentient beings of their own accord, from their own efforts, gain any little experience of happiness and joy here and there, we should be all the more grateful, because without our helping them, they have been able to achieve these joyful experiences and happiness.

(81) If I wish for all sentient beings to become
Buddhas worshipped throughout the three realms,
They why am I tormented
When I see them receiving mere mundane respect?

(82) If a relative for whom I am caring
And to whom I must give many things
Should be able to find his own livelihood,
Wouldn't I be happy, rather than angry?

Shantideva goes on to point out that a Bodhisattva practitioner has pledged to place all sentient beings at the highest state of existence, which is the state of Buddhahood, a state worthy of reverence from sentient beings in all three realms. If that is the case, how can such a practitioner allow himself or herself to be tormented by the perception of other people's success, joy, and happiness? Then he gives an example: if, for instance, there are people toward whom one is financially and materially responsible, who depend on one financially and materially, and if these people, of their own accord, can make their own livelihoods and succeed by themselves, then what happens is that this lightens one's burden toward them. Therefore in such situations one should feel grateful and happy that they can stand on their own feet and work for their own livelihood. Similarly, as a practitioner of bodhichitta who on a daily basis thinks about the well-being of all sentient beings and constantly prays for it, we have to bear in mind that when we say "all sentient beings," everyone without exception is included within that thought, even individuals whom one might dislike or find irritating, such as enemies, and so on.

> (83) If I do not wish for beings to have even this,
> How can I wish for them to awaken?
> And where is there an Awakening Mind
> In him who becomes angry when others receive things?

In this verse, Shantideva asks, "If I cannot tolerate or bear other people having material successes or material acquisitions and joy, then how can I claim that I wish them to become fully enlightened?" It is hypocritical. There is no way that bodhichitta can develop in such a person's mind.

> (84) What does it matter if (my enemy) is given something
>   or not?
> Whether he obtains it

Or whether it remains in the benefactor's house,
In either case I shall get nothing.

Here, Shantideva notes that when one's enemy acquires certain material benefit, let us say from a benefactor, there is no point in being jealous, nor is there any point in feeling dislike because of that. Even if our enemy does not receive that material thing from his or her benefactor, it is not going to make any difference so far as we ourselves are concerned: if our enemy does not receive that material thing, it is not going to be given to us. So as far as we are concerned, whether that material thing is given to our enemy or remains in the home of the benefactor, the friend of the enemy, makes no difference.

(85) So why, by becoming angry, do I throw away my merits,
The faith (others have in me) and my good qualities?
Tell me, why am I not angry (with myself)
For not having the causes for gain?

(86) Let alone not having any remorse
About the evils that you committed, (O mind,)
Why do you wish to compete with others
Who have committed meritorious deeds?

In fact, what one truly desires is material wealth or success; feeling jealous of others' success and others' material wealth is totally inappropriate. Because of that jealousy, one in fact destroys one's own virtuous roots or imprints, which in the future would lead to material success, acquisition of material wealth, and so on. So if one is serious in the aspiration to attain material possessions, then one should feel all the more angry toward oneself, the person who feels jealous of others' material success.

Further, Shantideva says that when we see our enemy being successful, acquiring material possessions, and when others speak highly of him or her, instead of feeling jealous and feeling bitter or angry about it, if we, in fact, rejoice in their success, if we feel joyful and happy, there's a possibility that we will be able to share in the success. Maybe there is that possibility. However, he says, by being jealous and angry about these successes, one is not only failing in one's ability to develop a deep sense of regret for the negative actions committed in the past, one is in some sense aggressively competing with the consequences of virtuous deeds committed by others.

> (87) Even if your enemy is made unhappy
> What is there for you to be joyful about?
> Your merely wishing (for him to be hurt)
> Did not cause him to be injured.

> (88) And even if he does suffer as you had wished,
> What is there for you to be joyful about?
> If you say, "For I shall be satisfied,"
> How could there be anything more wretched than that?

> (89) This hook cast by the fishermen of disturbing
>   conceptions
> Is unbearably sharp: Having been caught on it,
> It is certain that I shall be cooked
> In cauldrons by the guardians of hell.

In the first of these three verses, Shantideva asks the question, if our enemy is made unhappy, even through our action, what is there for us to be joyful about? Simply wishing to hurt someone, simply wishing something bad for our enemy is not, in any case, causing any harm or injury to that enemy. Even if by our wishful thinking all the negative things, all the failures or problems that we wished for our enemy did take place, what would there be to rejoice about? If we say, "Well, in that case, I would feel very satisfied," then Shantideva says, "How can there be anything more wretched than that?"

He concludes by stating that this anger or hatred is like a fisherman's hook, so it is very important for us to be cautious and ensure that we are not caught by this hook of hatred.

> (90) The honor of praise and fame
> Will not turn into merit or life;
> It will give me neither strength nor freedom from sickness,
> And will not provide any physical happiness.

> (91) If I were aware of what held meaning for me,
> What value would I find in these things?
> If all I want is (a little) mental happiness,
> I should devote myself to gambling, drinking, and so forth.

Then, in verses 90 and 91, Shantideva points out that we should not be too concerned with our fame or what people say about us, either bad or good, because in reality fame would not make any serious difference to one's life. Therefore, we should have our priorities right, and seek what is truly of value, what is truly of meaning to our life, not just mere fame, which is, after all, empty sounds. One might respond to this by saying, "This is not true, because when I enjoy fame and people speak highly of me, it gives me a lot of satisfaction." There is a kind of immediate gratification. But if that is one's sole purpose, then, as Shantideva indicates, on that ground one can also justify drinking all the time, or using substances such as drugs, because they too provide instant gratification.

> (92) If for the sake of fame
> I give away my wealth or get myself killed,
> What can the mere words (of fame) do then?
> Once I have died, to whom will they give pleasure?

Here, Shantideva explains that sometimes we do find cases in which individuals would, in fact, sacrifice many of their material possessions, wealth, and so forth, just for the sake of fame. And we also find cases in which individuals go to such an extent to acquire fame that they would even sacrifice their own lives for it. If we examine these cases, we find that in reality the individual does not benefit from the fame. After all, fame is nothing but empty words, empty sounds, and once the individual has died, who is there to benefit from it? The very purpose of seeking fame was to gain a sense of satisfaction. Yet if life itself is sacrificed for it, then there is no one to benefit. So this type of obsession with seeking fame is very childish and is quite foolish. People can get completely drunk with the idea of fame.

> (93) When their sandcastles collapse,
> Children howl in despair;
> Likewise when my praise and reputation decline
> My mind becomes like a little child.

In this verse, Shantideva presents an analogy: when children playing on the beach build sandcastles, they take it so seriously that when the sandcastle collapses they howl and cry. People who are drunk with fame are acting in a similar manner.

> (94) Since short-lived sounds are inanimate
> They cannot possibly think of praising me.
> —But as it makes (the bestower of praise) happy,
> (My) reputation is a source of pleasure (for me)—

> (95) But whether this praise is directed at myself or
>   someone else
> How shall I be benefitted by the joy (of him who
>   bestows it)?
> Since that joy and happiness are his alone
> I shall not obtain even a part of it.

> (96) But if I do find happiness in his happiness
> Then surely I should feel the same way towards all?

And if this were so then why am I unhappy
When others find pleasure in that which brings them joy?

(97) Therefore the happiness that arises
From thinking, "I am being praised," is invalid.
It is only the behavior of a child.

In these four verses, Shantideva explains that if one closely examines what it is that makes us happy when people speak highly of us, it is not fame itself. It is not the sound, because sounds are quite momentary and, in some sense, motiveless. The sounds by themselves do not have the intention to please us, nor do they have affection toward us. Now, we may think that when someone praises us or speaks highly of us, at that instant, at least in the mind or in the heart of that person who is praising us, there is a sense of joy, a sense of satisfaction, a sense of fulfillment. That's why I feel happy when people speak highly of me. But if that is the case, so far as the happiness that exists in the mind of the person who is praising is concerned, it remains in the heart of that person, it is not part of our mental continuum. So how can we, in reality, take part in that joy, in that happiness? And if we respond that this is not the whole point, the point is that by the simple act of someone praising me, it gives the opportunity for one person to be happy and joyful, i.e., the person who praises me, then why should we not also feel the same way when someone praises our enemy? At least in the mind or heart of the person who is praising our enemy, there is a sense of joy and happiness. So in verse 97, he concludes that the happiness or joy that arises from thinking, "I am being praised," is itself invalid. It is only the behavior of a child.

(98) Praise and so forth distract me
And also undermine my disillusion (with cyclic existence);
I start to envy those who have good qualities
And all the very best is destroyed.

(99) Therefore, are not those who are closely involved
In destroying my praise and the like
Also involved in protecting me
From falling into the unfortunate realms?

Here, Shantideva points out that in fact there are many destructive consequences or disadvantages of being praised by others. The first is that when one becomes very famous, when people begin to praise and speak highly of one, it will cause a lot of distraction in one's practice, because when one becomes very famous, one becomes very busy and has no time. Not only that, but it also may undermine one's dissatisfaction with unenlightened existence, because as one becomes famous everything seems to look quite all right. Then, when one thinks of samsaric existence, one may think, "Oh, it's not bad. It's quite joyful." There is a danger that when one reads about the faults and defects of samsaric existence, one may think, "Oh, maybe this was written by impoverished meditators living in far isolated places. They knew nothing about the reality of the world." So there is that danger of undermining one's appreciation of the unsatisfactory nature of cyclic existence. Then, third, as one becomes famous and people praise one, it may go to one's head and one may feel very proud. As one's pride increases, one becomes quite arrogant because one is successful in the eyes of the world. Although one might see jealousy among beggars, jealousy seems to be stronger when one becomes successful; somehow the intensity of jealousy increases with increasing success.

So these are the potential dangers of being praised by others. One should reflect upon these, because through these factors, ultimately, one's own spiritual progress can be hampered.

(100) I who am striving for freedom
Do not need to be bound by material gain and honor.
So why should I be angry
With those who free me from this bondage?

(101) Those who wish to cause me suffering
Are like Buddhas bestowing waves of blessing.
As they open the door for my not going to an unfortunate
    realm,
Why should I be angry with them?

Generally speaking, we find in Buddhist literature a description
of the ideal form of human existence, which is endowed with
what are known as the eight qualities that make one's existence
full and complete. These include possessing material wealth and
being successful in the world, and so on. These are seen as favorable
conditions; if one can use them constructively, then they can be
very useful. They can assist the individual not only on his or her
spiritual path, but also will make him or her all the more effective
when working for the benefit of other sentient beings. However,
while one possesses the facilities of wealth, position, education, and
so on, it is crucial that there be some internal restraining factor that
constantly keeps one in check so one is not spoiled by these facilities and never loses the fundamental insight into the underlying
unsatisfactory nature of cyclic existence. In that case, one's attitude
toward all these facilities will be in its proper perspective, i.e., to
be utilized as an aid in the path and for working for the benefit of
other sentient beings. There is always the need to maintain balance, not to go to any extremes, and at the same time to have full
knowledge of how to proceed along the path in the best and most
effective way.

If one is aware of these facts, then it is possible to view the individuals who get in the way of one's acquiring material successes,
material wealth, fame, position, and so on, not as enemies but
rather as protectors who keep one from the potential dangers of
being spoiled and obstructed from the path toward enlightenment.

So, in verses 100 and 101, Shantideva reminds us that we should
never lose sight of our ultimate goal. Our ultimate aspiration is
to attain freedom from suffering—liberation, or nirvana. So we
should not let ourselves become bound by material gain and honor.

Therefore, why should we be angry toward those such as our enemies who obstruct our material acquisitions and so on, and are, in fact, helping to free us from this bondage? Shantideva states that what these people are doing is like the blessings of Buddha, because through their acts they are protecting us from entering into the house that leads to the room of unfortunate existence. They are, in a sense, putting a lock on the door which would otherwise lead us to suffering. Therefore, one should not feel angry toward these people.

> (102) —But what if someone should obstruct my gaining
>   merit?—
> With him too it is incorrect to be angry;
> For since there is no fortitude similar to patience
> Surely I should put it into practice.

In verse 102, Shantideva responds to the feeling that if one's enemy, through his or her action, causes one's own merit or virtue to be destroyed, then one is justified in being angry. This too is not adequate justification for being angry toward one's enemy, he answers, because the best practice for accumulating merit or creating virtuous imprints is the practice of love and compassion. That is the true Dharma practice. In order to become fully successful in practicing love and compassion, a practice of patience and tolerance is indispensable. Therefore, there is no fortitude similar to patience; there is no practice greater than patience. One must not be angry toward the enemy's acts, but one should use the opportunity to enhance one's practice of patience and tolerance.

> (103) If due to my own failings
> I am not patient with this (enemy),
> Then it is only I who am preventing myself
> From practicing this cause for gaining merit.

Here, it is stated that even if I am given this opportunity, if due to my own failings I am not successful in being patient or tolerant toward my enemy and lose my temper, then it is only I myself who prevents me from using this opportunity to gain merit through the practice of patience. Therefore, in this sense, we ourselves destroy the cause of patience.

> (104) If without it something does not occur
> And if with it, it does come to be,
> Then since this (enemy) would be the cause of (patience)
> How can I say that he prevents it?

In this verse, Shantideva briefly defines what is meant by cause. He states that if without it something cannot occur, and if with it, it does come into being, then that is the cause of the event or action. In the case of patience, without an enemy's action there is no possibility for patience or tolerance to arise. Therefore, the enemy's action is an indispensable factor for our having the opportunity to practice patience. So how can we say the contrary, that the enemy prevents us from practicing patience? In fact, the enemy is the necessary condition for practicing patience.

> (105) A beggar is not an obstacle to generosity
> When I am giving something away,
> And I cannot say that those who give ordination
> Are an obstacle to becoming ordained.

Then Shantideva uses the example of a beggar who truly deserves to be given something. One cannot say such a beggar is an obstacle to practicing generosity. Similarly, how can one say the preceptor who gives ordination and vows is the obstacle for taking ordination?

> (106) There are indeed many beggars in this world,
> But scarce are those who inflict harm;
> For if I have not injured others
> Few beings will cause me harm.

> (107) Therefore, just like treasure appearing in my house
> Without any effort on my part to obtain it,
> I should be happy to have an enemy
> For he assists me in my conduct of Awakening.

In these two verses, Shantideva states that indeed there are many beggars in the world so that you can practice your generosity. However, in comparison, there are fewer opportunities for practicing patience. This is because in order for an enemy to inflict harm upon us, unless we provoke it, there is, generally speaking, no harm inflicted; it needs an interaction. So, when one comes across such an opportunity, one should treat it with gratitude. Like having found a treasure in one's own house, one should be happy and grateful toward one's enemy for providing that precious opportunity.

> (108) And because I am able to practice (patience) with him,
> He is worthy of being given
> The very first fruits of my patience,
> For in this way he is the cause of it.

In this verse, Shantideva points out that if we ever are successful in our practice of patience and tolerance, it is due to the combination of our own efforts and the opportunity provided by our enemy. Therefore, we should acknowledge that and dedicate the fruits of our practice of patience first for the benefit of our enemy.

> (109) —But why should my enemy be venerated?
> He has no intention for me to practice patience.—
> Then why venerate the sacred Dharma?
> (It too has no intention) but is a fit cause for practice.

Here, Shantideva acknowledges that one might think, "Why should I venerate my enemy, or acknowledge his or her contribution? There was no intention to give me this opportunity for practicing patience; there was no intention of helping me." If that were the case, then we should also not venerate the Dharma, one of the three jewels, because true Dharma refers to the cessation and the path. And so far as the cessation and the path are concerned, on their part, there is no intention to help us. Yet we consider them objects worthy of veneration and respect. So what is important here is the effect, not so much the intention on the part of the other factor.

> (110) —But surely my enemy is not to be venerated
> For he intends to cause me harm—
> But how could patience be practiced
> If, like doctors, people always strove to do me good?

> (111) Thus since patient acceptance is produced
> In dependence upon (one with) a very hateful mind,
> That person should be worthy of veneration just like the
>   sacred Dharma,
> Because he is a cause of patience.

In these two verses, Shantideva explains that one might think, "Yes, you are right regarding the Dharma cessations and the path, that there is no intention to help us, but we venerate them. But at least in the case of the enemy, on their part, they not only have no wish or intention to help us, but, in fact, have malicious intention to harm us. They want to harm us. Therefore they are definitely not worthy of veneration or respect."

Shantideva says that, in fact, the presence of this hateful mind in the enemy and the intention to hurt us is exactly what make the enemy's action unique. Otherwise, if it is just the actual act of hurting us that is crucial, then even doctors, without the intention of harming us, often adopt methods which are quite painful. Some of the doctors' treatment also may involve surgery. Nonetheless, we do not consider these acts harmful or the acts of an enemy because the intention on the part of the doctor was to help us. Therefore, it is exactly this intention to harm us willfully that makes the enemy unique and that gives us this precious opportunity to practice patience.

Therefore, in verse 111, he concludes that just as one venerates the sacred Dharma, one should also treat enemies as objects worthy of veneration because they are the cause of the practice of patience.

Meditation

Let us now use this silent session to meditate on the practice of tong-len, "giving and taking." First, visualize, on the one side, sentient beings who are in desperate need of help, who are in an unfortunate state of suffering. Then, on the other side, visualize yourself as the embodiment of a self-centered person who is quite indifferent to the well-being and needs of other sentient beings. Then, as a neutral observer, see how your natural feeling inclines toward the two; whether your natural feeling of empathy reaches out to the weaker sentient beings who are in need, or inclines more toward this embodiment of selfishness. Then, after that, focus your attention on the needy and desperate sentient beings, and direct toward them all your positive energy, mentally giving them your successes, virtuous collections, positive energies, and so on. Then take upon yourself their suffering, their problems, and their negativities.

For example, we can visualize an innocent, starving child from Somalia and see how we would respond naturally toward that sight. Here, when we generate deep empathy toward the suffering of that individual, it is not based on considerations such as, "He's my relative. She's my friend." You don't even know the person, but because of the fact that the other person is a human being, and you yourself are a human being, your natural capacity for empathy allows you to reach out. So you can visualize this way, and think that this child has no ability of his or her own to gain relief from the present state of difficulty. Then, mentally take upon yourself all the sufferings of starvation, poverty, and feelings of difficulty. Then, mentally give your own facilities, your successes, your wealth, and so on, to this child. So, engage in this give-and-take relationship. In this way, you train your mind. When you do the visualization of taking upon yourself, it is useful to visualize the sufferings, problems, and difficulties in the form of either poisonous substances or dangerous weapons—things that normally the very sight of makes you shudder. You could also visualize animals which you just can't stand the sight of. So visualize them in these forms and then absorb them directly into your heart. When you do that visualization effectively, it will make you feel a slight discomfort. That is an indication that it is hitting its target, that is, the self-centered, egocentric attitude that we normally have. However, for those individuals who may have problems with their own self-image, like having hatred or anger toward oneself and low self-esteem, it is important to judge for yourselves whether this particular practice is appropriate or not. It may not be.

Questions

Q: Shantideva writes as if the decision to develop bodhichitta or take the Bodhisattva path is one of pure intellect. Wherein do we listen to the heart?

A: We find in Buddhism discussion of three types of wisdom, or three stages in one's understanding. First is the stage of hearing or learning, the initial stage when you read or hear about something. Then as a result you immediately develop some sense of understanding. The second stage is when, after learning, or after having heard or read, you think about the issue or the topic constantly, and through constant familiarity and thinking, your understanding becomes clearer. Then at that time you begin to have certain feelings or experiences. The third stage is called the "meditatively acquired wisdom." This is when you not only intellectually understand the subject matter but also, through meditative experience, are able to feel it. So there is an assimilation of your knowledge with your experience.

At the initial stage, you can see a kind of difference, or gap, between the intellect and the object of knowledge, but at the meditatively acquired wisdom level, there is no gap; it is experiential knowledge. There may be a few exceptional cases in which some individuals do not have to go through this procedure, but generally speaking, for many of the Dharma practices, which do not come to us naturally, we need conscious effort on our part and need to go through these stages. In addition, these processes of understanding will make the subject matter much more experiential and close to the heart, as well as much more spontaneous.

This is analogous to the case of our delusory states, our afflictive emotions. Although in general afflictive emotions come about naturally, when directed to a particular object, for instance, when we have anger or hatred toward a person, if we leave them unattended, then there is less likelihood of their developing to an intense degree. Whereas if we think about the projected injustices done to us, the ways in which we have been unfairly treated, and we keep on thinking about them, that feeds on the hatred and makes it very powerful and intense. Similarly, when you have an attachment toward a particular person, then you can feed on that by thinking about how beautiful he or she is and then thinking about the projected qualities that you see in the person, and as you keep at this, the attachment becomes more and more intense. This also shows how through constant familiarity and thinking, afflictive emotions become more intense and powerful.

As I pointed out earlier, at the initial stage there is intelligence or understanding acquired through learning or hearing. This also includes reading. Then, as you ponder the subject, through thinking and analysis, you will get to a point where understanding begins to dawn. The Tibetan word is *nyamogtuchupa* (*nyams 'ogtu chudpa*), which means you feel as if you have grasped the subject. There is a sense of familiarity, a sense of affinity with the topic, so that it no longer appears alien to you. And then, again, as you pursue this process of familiarization you will get to a point where you develop a kind of experiential knowledge. That, in the technical language, is described as "the experience dependent upon effort." That type of experience requires conscious effort and exertion on your part. However as you pursue the topic still further, you will gradually get to a point where your experience becomes spontaneous, almost like second nature. Then you no longer need to go through the whole process of thinking and putting conscious effort into it. In the case of compassion, for example, where previously you might have had to go through the whole process of thinking, meditating, and so on, at this point the very sight of a suffering sentient being will give rise to a spontaneous, genuine compassionate state. That is the state known as "the spontaneous experience which is free of exertion."

So it seems there is this kind of progression from one stage to another. One should not have the notion that the spontaneity of one's experience goes totally in one direction and intellectual understanding goes in a totally different direction, as if they were completely separate and unrelated. That is a misconception. In fact, any understanding or experience that is developed through this process, through intellectual understanding and training, once you acquire it, is very stable and lasting. Compared to that, there may be some instances where you can have a spontaneous experience that seems very gripping and very powerful in the moment. But if it lacks intellectual grounding it will not be stable. After a few days, when the experience goes away, you will return to your ordinary, normal self without the experience having had much impact on you. So it is not reliable.

I think there may be different levels of experience. But according to my own experience, for example with bodhichitta, there were times these words appeared to be just words. Of course, I understood the meaning of the words at the linguistic level, but there was not much feeling. With regard to emptiness, *shunyata*, it was much the same. Of course I could explain something about the meaning of emptiness, but there was not much feeling associated with it. Then I thought about it year by year, for decades and decades. Then eventually these words, when I thought about them, became not just words, there was something more.

Q: As a mother of small children and mainstay of our household, my daily life has few free moments. My social environment is quite secular and not supportive of Dharma practice, though not hostile to it either. I am somewhat overwhelmed with the implications of adopting Dharma practice given my current circumstances, yet I want to make positive changes and apply effort toward developing mental discipline, bodhichitta, and wisdom. What would be your advice to a beginning practitioner for setting priorities for practice under these conditions?

A: Even in my case, if I wish to complain, I can always complain about lack of time. I am very busy. However if you make the effort, you can always find some time—say the early morning. Then, I think there are some times such as the weekend. You can sacrifice some of your fun. So if you make the effort and try hard enough, perhaps you may be able to find, let us say, thirty minutes in the morning, and thirty minutes in the evening. Maybe it is possible to figure out a way of getting some time. However, I feel it is very important first of all to develop a fairly general understanding, a kind of overview, of the basic Buddhist path.

If we think seriously and if we understand Dharma practice in the true sense of its meaning, then we should understand Dharma in terms of our mental state, i.e., our psychological and emotional state. One should not confine one's understanding of Dharma only to some physical or verbal activities, like doing recitations or chanting. If your understanding of Dharma practice is limited only to these activities, then of course you will need a specific time, a separate allotted time to do your practice, because you can't go around doing your daily chores like cooking and so on while reciting mantras. This could be quite annoying to people around you. However, if you understand Dharma practice in its true sense, then you will know that it has to do with psychological and emotional well-being. Therefore, you can use all twenty-four hours of your day for your practice.

For example, if you find yourself in a situation in which you might insult someone, then you immediately take precautions and restrain yourself from doing that. Similarly, if you encounter a situation in which you may lose your temper, immediately be mindful and say, "No, this is not the appropriate way." That is actually a practice of Dharma. Seen in that light, you will always have time.

Similarly, if you are meditating on the transient, momentarily changing nature of phenomena, then there are plenty of examples around you which will remind you of that fact. However what is important is first to study, because without knowledge it is difficult to practice.

Q: What should you say to a loved one who is talking about a third person with hatred or anger? On the one hand, you want to show compassion for the feelings being experienced by the loved one. On the other hand, you don't want to reinforce or lend approval to that hatred. What might one say?

A: Here I would like to tell a story. Once there was a Kadampa master called Gampowa who had many responsibilities. One day he complained to the Kadampa master Dromtonpa that he had hardly any time for his meditation or for his Dharma practice. So Dromtonpa responded by agreeing with him, "Yes, that's right. I don't have any time either." Then once an immediate affinity was established, Dromtonpa skillfully said, "But, you know what I am doing is for the service of the Dharma. Therefore, I feel satisfied." Similarly, if you find one of your beloved ones speaking against someone out of anger or hatred, maybe your initial reaction should be one of agreement and sympathy. Then once you have gained the person's confidence, you can say, "But. . . ."

Q: On this historic day with the signing of a peace agreement between the Israelis and the Palestinians, would you please comment on this momentous event, and perhaps offer a blessing for continuing peace in the Middle East as the difficult work begins?

A: Just as we had a discussion this morning, during which I commented that this event is something to be commended, you may be interested to know that I wrote a letter to both Prime Minister Rabin and PLO Chairman Yasser Arafat.

Q: Please explain skillful means more completely.

A: That's difficult. There are many different levels of methods. Gaining some understanding of what is meant by the wisdom factor is comparatively easy. The understanding of skillful means is much more difficult because it is so varied and so complex.

Generally speaking, one can define skillful means, or the method aspect of the path, as those practices, meditations, or aspects of the path that are principally associated with the conventional side of reality. We have conventional reality and ultimate reality, in other words, appearance and emptiness. And the techniques, meditations, and practices which are primarily associated with the ultimate nature of reality, that is, emptiness, can be described as the wisdom aspect of the path. Those which deal primarily with the appearance level, with the conventional aspect of reality, can be roughly defined as skillful means or the method aspect.

We also find that, generally speaking, many of the aspects of skillful means, or the method aspects of the path, such as love, compassion, and so on, are not cognitive. These are not cognitive in the sense that there is a greater involvement with the affective or emotional side of the psyche. The wisdom aspect has a more cognitive component that has more to do with one's apprehension or understanding. However, it is very difficult to come up with a detailed explanation of what exactly skillful means are.

Q: One Bodhisattva vow says to forgive someone who apologizes. What about forgiving someone who does not apologize? Is it desirable to ask for an apology from someone who has wronged you? What is the connection between forgiveness and patience?

A: The reason that Bodhisattvas are recommended to accept an apology when expressed by another is because if you don't accept another's apology, that will hurt the other person. The other person will think, "Oh, he or she still hasn't forgiven me." So this is done in order to protect the other person, to help the other person from feeling hurt. If the other person who has wronged you hasn't given any apology, there is no point in asking for it. Otherwise, you will be begging for that person to apologize. In fact, this will make the other person more uncomfortable.

Q: I have problems believing in reincarnation. What is the best approach which will lead me to believe in it?

A: This is very understandable, even for us Tibetans, who feel we have a very strong faith or belief in reincarnation or rebirth. But if we examine the content of our belief very carefully and honestly, then sometimes it becomes problematic because, unlike a belief in the solidity of material objects around us, where there is very concrete evidence for their existence and we can feel them, with matters like rebirth it is very difficult to have a concrete belief.

However, even among those people who are extremely skeptical of rebirth or who consciously deny its existence, if you ask them for the grounds upon which they reject it, or on what grounds they are extremely skeptical of it, then ultimately they will say, "I just don't feel like believing in it."

Generally speaking, we have two principal categories of philosophical systems: on the one hand, you have the whole camp which subscribes to belief in rebirth or reincarnation, and on the other, you have the camp which does not subscribe to belief in reincarnation or rebirth, or, in fact, denies its existence. But, in reality, if you examine it, it is not that the second group has found evidence which is counter to the existence of rebirth; rather, they haven't found any evidence confirming existence or belief. So, it is important to be able to distinguish between not having found evidence for something and having found evidence which disproves it. These are two different things.

Here there is the need to understand how we use proof or evidence, either in proving something or disproving it. We also have to understand the scope of a particular type of reasoning or argument. For instance, there are certain types of reasoning which state that if the phenomenon is such that if it were to exist, then we should be able to find it through a certain method of analysis. If the phenomenon belongs to that category, then subject it to analysis. If you don't find it, then you can use that as evidence that the phenomenon does not exist, because if it were to exist, you should be able to find it through these means. Then, there are other types of phenomena which may not fall into the scope of that form of reasoning.

Now as to the question of rebirth, it is something that has to be understood on the basis of a continuum of consciousness. You cannot account for it on the basis of the continuity of your bodily existence, let alone what happens to the consciousness after death. Even when you are alive, it is extremely difficult to identify what exactly the nature of consciousness is, and what its relationship with the body is, and whether or not there is a separate thing called "consciousness" which is not material. Or is consciousness a mere illusion? And so on. It is a very problematic area for which there are no clear, precise answers according to modern scientific discipline.

However, on the other hand, we also find exceptional individuals, even to this day, who are capable of recollecting experiences from their past lives. We also find that through meditation, some individuals have certain types of experiences which are very mysterious.

Day Four

Nagarjuna pays homage to Buddha Shakyamuni by praising him as the teacher who propounds the philosophy of emptiness—that all things and events are without intrinsic existence or intrinsic identity, and that although they lack identity and existence they still function in their ability to produce effects and so on. One can realize this through understanding the dependent or interdependent nature of reality. Nagarjuna pays homage to Buddha Shakyamuni, who propounded this doctrine of the emptiness of intrinsic reality by teaching the dependently arising nature of phenomena.

Generally speaking, we find in the Madhyamika literature various forms of reasoning which are aimed at establishing the absence of intrinsic existence and intrinsic identity of phenomena. These include trying to analyze how things arise nominally and conceptually; by analyzing that nature, we arrive at the conclusion that things lack intrinsic reality. Further, we find such forms of argument known as "examining the identity and difference of phenomena." We also find other types of arguments or reasoning which examine phenomena from the causal perspective, that is, from the perspective of their ability to produce effects and so on.

However, among all of these forms of reasoning, the most powerful is the reasoning of dependent origination, which is employed by Nagarjuna. When a particular thing or event is established by means of its dependently originating nature as being without intrinsic reality and intrinsic existence and identity, we find that we are not denying the existence of phenomena; we are trying to understand their existence and identity in terms of their relationships to other phenomena. In some sense, existence and identity can be said to emerge in relation to other phenomena.

What is so unique about this form of reasoning, which heavily relies upon the interdependent nature of reality, is that it has the capacity to arrive at the "middle way." This is a position free from the extreme of absolutism, because one is not holding on to some sort of intrinsic reality; yet at the same time, it is also free from the extreme of nihilism, because one is not denying the existence and identity of phenomena. One is accepting a formal existence which is dependent, which is emergent, and which is understood in terms of its interaction and interrelationship.

Therefore, in the *Entry into the Middle Way*, we find Chandrakirti stating that once one's understanding of the existence and identity of phenomena is developed on the basis of understanding the interdependent nature of reality and how identity and existence are in some sense derived through this interrelationship, then this allows one to understand the fundamental Buddhist concept of causality, in which our understanding of the nature of reality is derived from the appreciation of mere conditionality. In this way, one will be able to refute the idea of unproduced or uncaused phenomena, because things come into being through interaction with other factors, due to causes and conditions. And through this insight into the interdependent nature of reality, one will also be able to refute the idea of creation by some sort of absolute, independent being, because again, one's understanding of causality is in terms of mere conditionality. Similarly, one will be able to refute the idea that a thing may come into being by being dependent on causes which are identical to itself or are totally independent from itself. One will be able to free oneself from all these extremes and be able to accept the fundamental idea of causality in its true sense.

However, when we try to understand what is meant by mere conditionality, or how things and events come into being entirely in dependence on other causes and conditions, there are many problematic areas that we have to bear in mind.

Let us take for example our own aggregates, our own *skandhas*. If we look at the continuum of the most subtle aggregate, that is, consciousness, and also at the sense of "I" or "self," the personal identity is based on the continuum of the subtle aggregate, the general sense of "I" which is unqualified, either as a human being, or as a person of particular ethnic origin, or whatever—there is no qualification. The mere sense of "I" or mere identity, that "I" or sense of self which is derived from the continuum of the subtle aggregate, is beginningless, so far as its continuum is concerned. Therefore, that "self" or that "I" which is associated with our identity as a human being cannot be said to be specific to a single lifetime. We cannot say it is a human being; we cannot say it is an animal. But we can say this is a being.

In terms of its continuum, we can say that self together with the basis of that sense of self, which is the subtle aggregate, arises from its earlier moment, which arises from its earlier instance, and so forth, because there is a continuous process. However, we cannot say that it is a product of karma, because karma, in terms of its continuing process, has no role in making the process go on. It is simply a natural fact that this continuum carries on.

However, if one looks at a slightly grosser level, let us say at the level of human existence, then we have the human body and the human identity that leads one to say, "I am a human being." That sense of self, and the aggregates on which that identity is based, can be said to be a product of karma. This is because when we say "human body" and "human existence," we are talking about the consequence or fruit of positive karma, the virtuous actions which one has accumulated in the past. So it is there that karma plays a role.

Let us take the case of a human body. Although in general we can say it is a product of good karma, if we trace the material origin, the substantial cause which is the material origin of our body, we can trace it by means of the causal principle to its earlier instance of the parental regenerative fluids, then go further and further. Then we can trace the material origin until, let us take the example of this particular universal system, to a point where it is totally empty space. According to Buddhist cosmology, prior to the evolution of a particular universal system, all the material substances are believed to be inherent in what are known as "space particles." So again, as far as the process of the material continuum is concerned, it is a natural fact, a natural law, that the causal principle propels material substances to carry on their continuum. Again, there is no role for karma there.

Now the question is, at what point or at what stage does karma come into the picture? At the stage of empty space, the space particles will carry on their material continuum, which will give rise to various composite particle structures, leading to, according to scientific theory, molecular structure. Becoming more and more complex, there will come a point where the composition of the material particles will make a difference to individuals who inhabit the world. In other words, the material will become directly relevant to individuals' experience of pain and pleasure. It is at that stage, in my view, that karma begins to play a role. These are problematic areas which I want you to think about.

Because of this complexity, we find in the Buddhist literature various avenues of reasoning and four key principles which are believed to be embedded in the natural world. The first three are the principle of natural law, the principle of dependence, and the principle of functions. Then, based on these three principles, one can apply logic or reasoning, and that is the principle of logical proof. Unless one has certain bases which one can use, one cannot acquire reasoning or logic.

So one could say that the reason we can appreciate the laws of chemistry is because there are certain principles known as "the principle of dependence" and "the principle of functions." When certain material substances interact, they give rise to emergent properties. Then that will allow us to appreciate the functions they can perform collectively, through interaction, and thus we can appreciate the laws of chemistry.

Here we may ask the question, "Why is there in the natural

world, as if they are given, the material realm and the mental realm—the spiritual realm or the realm of consciousness?" There is no rational answer. It is simply a given fact.

In light of these philosophical considerations, we arrive at the conclusion that things and events ultimately lack intrinsic existence or intrinsic identity. They derive their existence and identity only in relation to other factors, causes, and conditions, and therefore, the apprehension which grasps at things and events as existing intrinsically, possessing intrinsic identity and status, is a state of ignorance. In fact, it is a state of misconception. Therefore, by generating insight into the empty nature of phenomena, we will be able to directly see through the illusion of this misconception, because this insight directly opposes the mode of apprehension of this misknowledge. As a result, that distorted state of mind can be removed or eliminated. On these grounds it is believed that not only ignorance, but also the derivative delusory states which are rooted in that fundamental ignorant state can ultimately be removed.

Carrying this discussion further, Maitreya, in his text the *Sublime Continuum*, gives three reasons on the basis of which one can conclude that the essence of Buddhahood permeates the minds of all sentient beings. First, he says that the Buddha's activities radiate in the heart of all sentient beings. Now this can be understood in two different ways: one is that we can understand that in every sentient being there is a seed of virtue, and one could see the seed of virtue as an act of the completely enlightened, compassionate Buddha. But one could also see it in deeper terms, that is, that all sentient beings possess the potential for perfection. Therefore, there is a kind of perfected being inherent within all sentient beings, radiating. So one can understand it in these ways. Second, so far as the ultimate nature of reality is concerned, there is total equality between the samsaric state and nirvana. Third, we all possess a mind which lacks intrinsic reality and independent existence, which allows us to then remove the negativities and delusory states that obscure it. For these three reasons, Maitreya concludes that all sentient beings possess the essence of Buddhahood.

However, in order to activate that seed which is inherent within our heart or mind, we must develop compassion. Through cultivating universal compassion, one will be able to activate that seed, and this makes the individual more inclined toward the Mahayana path. For that, the practice of patience and tolerance is crucial. So let us return to the subject of patience.

> (112) Therefore the Mighty One has said
> That the field of sentient beings is (similar to) a Buddhafield,
> For many who have pleased them
> Have thereby reached perfection.

Because of sentient beings, such as one's enemy, and people who cause injury and hurt, one has precious opportunities to practice patience and tolerance and accumulate great stores of merit. Therefore, Buddha spoke of the field of the Buddhas and the field of sentient beings as fields for accumulating merit. These are "fields" in the sense that they serve as sources or foundations from which we can accumulate merit.

> (113) A Buddha's qualities are gained
> From sentient beings and the Conquerors alike,
> So why do I not respect them
> In the same way as I respect the Conquerors?

In verse 112, Shantideva states that those who have appreciated this fact and then please sentient beings will thereby reach perfection. Since this is the case, we find that both Buddhas, the fully enlightened ones, and sentient beings are equal in terms of being factors or conditions leading us to perfection.

Why is it then that we discriminate between the two and revere the Buddhas, the fully enlightened ones, and not the sentient beings? Why do we not revere and respect the sentient beings and acknowledge their contribution?

In fact, if we examine this carefully, we will find that there are more opportunities for accumulating great stores of merit through our interactions with sentient beings than through our interactions with the Buddha. With respect to the Buddha, we can accumulate merit by generating faith and confidence, making offerings, and so on. However, many of the practices that lead to enhancing our stores of merit can happen only in relation to other sentient beings. This is true even in terms of attaining a favorable rebirth in the future, for which we need to practice and have a way of life that is ethically disciplined, in which we restrain our body, speech, and mind from indulging in negative or nonvirtuous actions, such as killing, sexual misconduct, stealing, telling lies, and so on. These actions all depend on other beings; we cannot practice them in a vacuum.

In addition, when we obtain a favorable form of existence, such as a human body, even many qualities of the human body that we would consider desirable, such as a pleasant appearance, having material wealth, and so on, are also the consequences of virtuous deeds. For example, a pleasant appearance is the consequence of patience and tolerance, and material wealth is the consequence of the practice of generosity. Even these practices become possible only when there are other sentient beings. They cannot occur in a vacuum.

This is the case with the limited purpose of obtaining a favorable rebirth; it is even truer in terms of the path for obtaining full liberation from samsara, in which we need to practice many other things. For instance, in order to attain full enlightenment we need to practice love, compassion, and many other aspects of the path. In all of these, we find that unless there is an interaction with other sentient beings, there is no possibility of even beginning.

So we find that if we compare Buddhas and sentient beings in terms of their contribution to our acquiring stores of merit, sentient beings in fact seem to have a greater contribution than the Buddhas.

Now, let us take the example of generating insight into the nature of emptiness. That wisdom is very powerful, and is something that we practitioners must aspire to realize. However, if that insight is not complemented with the factor of method, that is, bodhichitta, then no matter how powerful that realization of emptiness may be, it can never reach a stage at which it can directly serve as an antidote for eliminating obstructions to knowledge.

Even in terms of enjoying a conventionally understood joyful and happy life, as I said earlier, we need certain factors, such as good health. Here again, in order to enjoy good health, other sentient beings have a great role because one needs to acquire the merit necessary to obtain that. Then, if we closely examine the material facilities that we use for our enjoyment of life, we find that there are hardly any material objects which have no sources in other people. All these facilities, if one thinks carefully, come into being as a result of the efforts of many people; either directly or indirectly, many people are involved in making them possible.

Similarly, in order to enjoy a happy life we need good companions, a circle of friends. When we talk about friends and companions, we speak of interaction with other human beings. While the relationships might involve hardships, like a lot of quarrels and cursing, in spite of all of this we have to try to maintain friendships and lead a way of life in which there is enough interaction with others in order to be happy. So here we see that even these three factors—good health, material possessions, and friendship—are all inextricably linked with other people's efforts and cooperation.

So if we think along these lines, we will find that not only in our ordinary state, but also when we are on the path as well as when we are at the resultant state of Buddhahood, even though Buddhas are fully enlightened beings and may be very sacred, very precious, and very highly realized beings, in terms of kindness and their contribution toward our well-being, it seems as if sentient beings have a greater role. So we should be more grateful toward sentient beings than toward Buddhas.

From another point of view, we can see that the Buddhas, the fully enlightened beings, have completely perfected their own self-realization. Therefore, to put it bluntly, they have nothing to do other than serve sentient beings. In a way, it's their duty. In some sense it's nothing to be admired or be surprised about: Buddhas work for the benefit of sentient beings. However, when we consider sentient beings, with all their weaknesses, faults, and intact delusory states of mind, afflictive emotions, and so on, even with these limitations their contribution toward our well-being cannot be underestimated. Therefore, we should feel all the more grateful to them.

One can think along these lines and ask, "Who is kinder to us—the Buddhas or sentient beings?" In response, the statements made here in the *Guide to the Bodhisattva's Way of Life*, when one thinks carefully about them, are not really exaggerations.

So what is meant by equality of the Buddhas and sentient beings? Here Shantideva says that the equality is not in terms of their realization, but rather in terms of being indispensable to our endeavors in accumulating merit and in attaining enlightenment. In this regard, both Buddhas and sentient beings are equal.

(114) (Of course) they are not similar in the quality of their intentions
But only in the fruits (that they produce);
So it is in this respect that they have excellent qualities
And are therefore (said to be) equal.

(115) Whatever (merit comes from) venerating one with a loving mind
Is due to the eminence of sentient beings.
And in the same way the merit of having faith in Buddha
Is due to the eminence of Buddha.

(116) Therefore they are asserted to be equal
In the share they have in establishing Buddha-qualities.
But none of them are equal (in good qualities)
With the Buddhas who are boundless oceans of excellence.

(117) Even if the three realms were offered,
It would be insufficient in paying veneration

To those few beings in whom a mere share of the good
    qualities
Of the Unique Assemblage of Excellence appears.

(118) Thus since sentient beings have a share
In giving rise to the supreme Buddha-qualities,
Surely it is correct to venerate them
As they are similar in merely this respect?

In these verses, Shantideva points out that if we consider bodhi-chitta and a good heart as objects worthy of veneration, then we should also consider sentient beings worthy of veneration, because the greatness of bodhichitta and a good heart comes from the greatness of sentient beings. If we consider merits such as those acquired through having faith toward the Buddha as virtuous, then that is due to the greatness of the Buddha. Therefore, Buddhas and sentient beings are asserted to be equal. In fact, sentient beings' contribution cannot be reimbursed or reciprocated even if we were to offer material goods filling all three realms to the Buddhas. He concludes that therefore, at least from the point of view of their kindness toward us, there is an adequate ground on which we should venerate sentient beings and respect them.

(119) Furthermore, what way is there to repay (the Buddhas)
Who grant immeasurable benefit
And who befriend the world without pretension,
Other than by pleasing sentient beings?

(120) Therefore since benefitting these beings will repay
Those who give their bodies and enter the deepest hell for
    their sake,
I shall behave impeccably in all (that I do)
Even if they cause me a great deal of harm.

(121) When for their sake, those who are my Lords
Have no regard even for their own bodies,
Then why am I the fool so full of self-importance?
Why do I not act like a servant towards them?

(122) Because of their happiness the Conquerors are
   delighted.
But if they are harmed they are displeased.
Hence by pleasing them I shall delight the Conquerors
And by harming them I shall hurt the Conquerors.

In these four verses, Shantideva argues that if we are serious
in our desire to repay the kindness of the Buddhas and venerate
them, there is no better way than pleasing sentient beings. In fact,
the well-being and interests of sentient beings are very dear to the
hearts of the fully enlightened ones. So much so that if one serves
sentient beings, the Buddhas will be pleased; and if one hurts them,
the Buddhas will be displeased. Therefore, if one is serious about
pleasing the Buddhas through one's meritorious actions, the best
way to achieve that is by paying respect to and acknowledging the
kindness of other sentient beings. He sums that up by stating,

(123) Just as desirable sense-objects would give my mind no
   pleasure
If my body was ablaze with fire,
Likewise, when living creatures are in pain,
There is no way for the Compassionate Ones to be pleased.

The next three verses read:

(124) Therefore, as I have caused harm to living beings,
Today I openly declare all my unwholesome deeds
That have brought displeasure to the Compassionate Ones,
Please bear with me, O Lords, for this displeasure I have
   caused you.

(125) From now on, in order to delight the Tathagatas,
I shall serve the universe and definitely cease (to cause
    harm).
Although many beings may kick and stamp upon my head,
Even at the risk of dying, may I delight the Protectors of the
    World by not retaliating.

(126) There is no doubt that those with the nature of
    compassion
Regard all these beings (as being the same) as themselves.
Furthermore, those who see (this Buddha-nature) as the
    nature of sentient beings see the Buddhas themselves;
Why then do I not respect (sentient beings)?

Then he concludes:

(127) (Pleasing living beings) delights the Tathagatas
And perfectly accomplishes my own purpose as well.
In addition, it dispels the pain and misery of the universe.
Therefore, I should always practice it.

These practices and reflections could also be applied by those
who believe in the concept of creation and Creator, by substituting
God for Buddhas or fully enlightened beings. This is because if one
is truly serious about living a way of life that would be in accordance with God's wishes, and that would please God and uphold
the principle of loving God, then the true indication of that would
be manifested in the way one deals with other sentient beings, at
least one's fellow human beings. Therefore, one's ideal of a truly
loving God must translate in one's behavior toward one's fellow
human beings.

In the Christian understanding, one's relationship to God takes
place within the framework of a single lifetime. There is no idea
of previous lives, but rather the belief that one's individual life is
created by God. As a result, there is less distance, and a kind of

intimacy in the relationship; there is a closeness about it. When one applies these practices within that framework, surely there would be a certain effect, something quite powerful in governing one's behavior and way of life.

I will read the remaining verses.

> (128) For example, should some of the king's men
> Cause harm to many people,
> Farsighted ones would not return the harm
> Even if they were able (to do so).

> (129) For they see that (these men) are not alone
> But are supported by the might of the king.
> Likewise, I should not underestimate
> Weak beings who cause me a little harm.

> (130) For they are supported by the guardians of hell
> And by all the Compassionate Ones.
> So (behaving) like the subjects of that fiery king,
> I should please all sentient beings.

> (131) Even if such a king were to become angry,
> Could he cause the pain of hell,
> Which is the fruit I would have to experience
> By displeasing sentient beings?

> (132) And even if such a king were to be kind,
> He could not possibly grant me Buddhahood,
> Which is the fruit I would obtain
> By pleasing sentient beings.

> (133) Why do I not see
> That my future attainment of Buddhahood,
> As well as glory, renown, and happiness in this very life
> All come from pleasing sentient beings?

And the final verse reads:

(134) While in cyclic existence, patience causes
Beauty, health, and renown.
Because of these, I shall live for a very long time
And win the extensive pleasure of the universal Chakra
      Kings.

This concludes "Patience," the sixth chapter of Shantideva's *Guide to the Bodhisattva's Way of Life*.

Meditation

Let us meditate on thoughtlessness—but not a mere state of dullness, or a "blanked-out" state of mind. Rather, you should first of all generate the determination required to maintain a state of thoughtlessness. Generally speaking, our mind is predominantly directed toward external objects. Our attention and our focus follow after our sense experiences, and remain at a sensorial and conceptual level. So withdraw your mind inward, not letting it chase after sensory objects. At the same time, not being so totally withdrawn that there is a kind of dullness, you should maintain a very full state of alertness and mindfulness. Then try to see this natural state of your consciousness in which it is not afflicted by thoughts of the past, things that have happened, memories, and so on; nor is it afflicted by thoughts of your future, such as future plans, anticipations, fears, and hopes. Rather, try to remain in the natural state.

This is a bit like a river which is flowing quite strongly, in which you cannot see the bed of the river clearly. If there was some way you could put an immediate stop to the flow from the direction the water is coming from and the direction the water is flowing to, then you could keep the water still, and that would allow you to see the bed quite clearly.

Similarly, when you are able to stop your mind from chasing

after sensory objects and when you can free your mind from being totally "blanked out," then you will begin to see under this turbulence of the thought processes a kind of underlying stillness, an underlying clarity of mind. You should try to do this, even though it is very difficult at the initial stage. Especially at the outset, since there is no specific object to focus on, there is a danger of falling asleep.

At the initial stage, when you begin to experience the natural state of consciousness, it will be in the form of some sort of vacuity, absence, or emptiness. This is because we are so habituated to understanding our mind in terms of external objects that we tend to look at the world through our concepts, images, and so on. So when you withdraw your mind from external objects, it's almost as if you can't recognize your mind. There's a kind of absence, a kind of vacuity. However, as you slowly progress and get used to it, you will begin to see an underlying clarity, a sort of luminosity. That's when you begin to appreciate and realize the natural state of the mind.

However, that state should not be confused with the realization of emptiness, or meditation on emptiness. Nor should you have the illusion this is a very profound meditative experience. This is something that is common to non-Buddhists and Buddhists alike, especially in the meditations of high levels of concentration, which are technically called "the formless states of mind," space-like, limitless, infinite consciousness. These are various levels of consciousness in which there is a kind of single-pointedness and stability, and where the stability and stillness are even more powerful. But again, these are not very profound meditative states. It is true, however, that many of the profound meditative experiences come from a basis of this kind of stillness of mind.

Begin the meditation with a simple breathing exercise. Focusing on the right and left nostrils, do three rounds of breathing, and focus your attention simply on the breath. Just be aware of inhaling, exhaling, and then inhaling, exhaling, three times. Then, start the meditation.

QUESTIONS

Q: Your Holiness and other teachers admonish us to be sincerely joyful about others' worldly achievements, happiness, and acquisitions as discussed in chapter six of Shantideva and in *The Path to Bliss*. If, however, we know with certainty that a person has acquired or achieved something through unskillful or nonvirtuous means, such as lying, stealing, cheating, harming, in what manner should that happiness for them be experienced and expressed?

A: You are right that one's attitude toward superficial successes that are achieved through wrong means of livelihood such as lying, stealing, cheating, and so on, should not be the same as for achievements and happiness which are genuine. However, here you must bear in mind that if you examine this carefully, you will find that although the immediate circumstances that gave rise to a person's joy and happiness may be a wrong means of livelihood, that is merely the immediate circumstance: the actual cause of that happiness is the individual's merit in the past. So one has to see the difference between immediate circumstances and long-term causes.

One of the characteristics of karmic theory is that there is a definite, commensurate relationship between cause and effect. There is no way that negative actions or unwholesome deeds can result in joy and happiness. Joy and happiness, by definition, are the results or fruits of wholesome actions. So, from that point of view, it is possible for us to admire not so much the immediate action, but the real causes of joy.

Q: In cases of injustice, do we accept it and use it for our patience, or attempt to change the structure of society which caused it? Where is the balance?

A: Yes, definitely, you must take the initiative to change the situation. I have no doubt.

Shantideva's teaching, although written many centuries ago, should be considered a source of strength for today, in order to change our society. Shantideva is not advising us to remain totally submissive and passive and not do anything. Rather, we should generate patience and tolerance, and use that as a strength for then changing the situation.

Q: After someone has wronged me, I remember this, and I think about it later and get angry again and again. How can I keep from doing this?

A: As I usually point out, in thinking about the person who caused this anger in you, if you look at it from a different angle, that person surely will have a lot of other positive qualities. Furthermore, if you look carefully, you will find that the event to which you initially responded with anger has also given you certain opportunities, something which otherwise would not have been possible, even from your point of view. So you can see many different angles to a single event. However if in spite of your efforts you do not find any such perspectives on this particular person's act, then for the time being the best course may be simply to try to forget about it.

Q: Would Your Holiness comment further on the relationship between the realization of emptiness, dependent arising, and patience? Would the practice of patience without the realization of emptiness and dependent arising always remain superficial?

A: Here, what we mean by the word "superficial" can again be seen from different perspectives. From the perspective of a more profound level of practice, then any practice of patience which is divorced from its complementary factor of wisdom and understanding of emptiness will remain, in some sense, superficial, because it may not be able to root out anger and hatred completely. However, that is not to say that we have to wait until we have realization of emptiness to start practicing patience. That is not the implication.

We find mentioned even in the Mahayana literature itself that there are many bodhisattvas who have great realizations but no realization of emptiness. The problem is, if we were to search for such a bodhisattva, it might be quite difficult to find one. I think, among Tibetans, there are some people who really have a deep experience of bodhichitta. Then among my friends there is one, I think, who has actually achieved the state of calm abiding. And according to him, he achieved calm abiding within four months, which is something quite amazing. But then, he also told me that he finds it difficult to develop bodhichitta. So he is not showing any keen interest in Tantrayana, because without bodhichitta the practice of Tantrayana is meaningless. So in my conversation with him, I discussed my practice a little bit. You see, because we became very close friends, he told me about his experiences. Otherwise, these people never show off. People such as myself who have no experience sometimes like showing off.

Q: Is it possible for a student to have a Tibetan teacher and only see that teacher once or twice a year?

A: It is very possible, but as I pointed out earlier, what is crucial is to see that this person possesses the minimum qualifications of a teacher. What is also important is to reserve only the most important questions for the teacher and not to ask silly questions.

Q: If certain conditions, delusions, or influences cause an individual to do harm to others, and/or act irrationally, when *is* it justified for this individual to be punished or imprisoned by others for that action?

A: Here, I feel it may be important to make distinctions between punishment in the form of prevention, and punishment simply as retribution for the act committed. It seems there are justifications for punishing someone as a means of preventing similar actions in the future.

This reminds me of the death penalty. It is, I feel, very, very sad that it still exists. Some nations actually prohibit it and stop the death sentence. This, I feel, is very good.

Q: In the large cities, many of the people we meet are strangers whom we meet only once and never see again. There is much indifference. Is there a special technique for compassion for this kind of brief meeting?

A: In order to generate a feeling of compassion and love toward another person, it is not presupposed that you need to know that person. If that were the case, then there would be no possibility of generating universal compassion because of the sheer number of sentient beings, until you became fully enlightened in the first place.

This is analogous to generating realization of the dynamic, transient nature of all phenomena. If that realization required being familiar with each and every single thing and event, then it would be impossible. However, it is possible through a universal approach to see that all things and events which come into being due to causes and conditions are impermanent and are transient, and so on. So you can adopt a much more universal approach and then realize their impermanent nature. Similarly, you can think that all experiences which are products of contaminated actions are ultimately unsatisfactory. For that realization, you don't need to go through each and every experience and think, "This is unsatisfying, this is unsatisfying, that is unsatisfying." You can generate that realization in a more universal way.

Similarly when generating universal compassion, you can generate compassion for all sentient beings in a universal way by thinking that all beings who have the capacity for feeling pain and pleasure, who regard their life as precious, have this innate, instinctive wish to be happy and overcome suffering. Therefore, I wish that they fulfill this aspiration and that I may be able to assist them. In that way, one can generate universal compassion.

Q: If one is studying and practicing Lam Rim and Dzogchen, is there a necessity or a purpose in yidam yoga, or Anuttara Yoga Tantra?

A: In order to engage in the meditation of Dzogchen, it requires preliminary empowerment and blessings which are associated with the practices of Highest Yoga Tantra. So without the practice of Highest Yoga Tantra, you cannot undertake a successful practice of Dzogchen. It may be possible that certain teachers, when giving instructions on Dzogchen and the preliminary practices, may not identify that this practice belongs to a particular tantra. However, when one considers the distinctions between *Maha*, *Anu*, and *Ati*, the three inner yogas in the Nyingma terminology, one has to understand that these three divisions are in fact divisions within Highest Yoga Tantra.

Q: Would His Holiness explain the role of solitude in achieving enlightenment? How is it similar to a monastic environment?

A: In fact, some of the monasteries are very busy and active, I think a bit to the extreme. In the past, there were great meditators living in the monasteries, in fact, some people that some of my friends have known. In order to engage in intensive practices in a more isolated way, one of the techniques these meditators used was to arrange a particular system of locking their door so they could take the key from the inside. In this way, from the outside it looked as if the person was not in. That way, they could keep the privacy and the solitude they were seeking. Some of these meditators have, in fact, advanced to a very high level of realization. Indeed, some of them have attained what is called the completion stage in Highest Yoga Tantra.

The Tibetan word for monastery is *gompa* (Tib. *dgon pa*), which etymologically contains the idea that it is a place of solitude set apart from the town. Because of that, in Tibet, in some of the monasteries, there were strict regulations that within the monastery one could not keep dogs because they would bark and make noises; one could not even ring bells for ritual purposes, no cymbal playing, no hand drum playing, no beating of drums. The only sound was people discussing Dharma in the debating courtyards. Other than that, there was a strict prohibition of any noise-making activities.

These days, unfortunately, it seems that people have the impression that if in a monastery there are no ritual performances, such as someone beating drums, or playing cymbals, or ringing bells, then it seems as if this monastery is not complete. That is a very wrong impression and is unfortunate. Monasteries must be filled with meditation and self-discipline in the meditation. Without that it's just like any other institution.

Q: What should I consider in trying to decide whether I should take the Bodhisattva vows at this time? I want to avoid the downfalls and practice the six perfections, but wonder whether I am capable.

A: Tomorrow, I will perform the ceremony for taking Bodhisattva vows, preceded by a ceremony of generating bodhichitta, which is different from taking vows. So in your case, it may be more advisable not to take the Bodhisattva vows, but to generate bodhichitta.

I don't know your particular situation, but if you are someone who has had exposure to Buddhism in general, and particularly Mahayana Buddhism, and has given a lot of thought to many of the practices of Mahayana, it may be different. Otherwise, if it is the first time you are being exposed to this kind of practice, Bodhisattva practice, then perhaps it is wiser not to take Bodhisattva vows at this point.

Q: What should the sangha collectively and individually do to serve others?

A: This is a very difficult issue because for the monks and nuns in the West, and particularly for the nuns, there is no established, reliable support system. So it is an issue that we must pay attention to and give a lot of thought to. However, individually, if monks and nuns can make any contribution to the society in general, then that is very admirable and wonderful, because, in fact, that is the very purpose of one's spiritual endeavor.

Like our Christian brothers and sisters: Christian monks and nuns are heavily involved in and committed to the service of society, mainly in the field of education, but also in the health field. This is really wonderful. Traditionally, among Buddhist monks and nuns, that kind of practice is still minimal. So, as soon as we came to India—I think, in early '60 or '61—I urged the authorities of our monasteries and nunneries that our monks and nuns eventually should carry out more work in these two fields. But, so far, there has been little response.

Then, there are Western Buddhist monks and nuns. Although there are some institutions here and there in Europe and Australia and many other places, still, at the moment, everywhere, you will find some difficulties. Of course, it will take time.

So I really admire those Western monks and nuns who, in spite of many difficulties, keep their vows and enthusiasm. Last March, we had a very fruitful meeting at Dharamsala; many nuns also participated, and some are here. They explained their difficulties. Their explanation made me cry. They are very efficient in that they are capable of piercing the hearts of their audience.

Q: Could you give advice to the person who comes to Buddhism late in life and starts practicing and studying the complexity of scriptures?

A: Don't worry. We have a historical precedent here from which you can draw strength and encouragement. During the time of the Buddha, there was a householder called Pelgye. At the age of eighty, he decided to take serious interest in Dharma practice. As a result, he was insulted and derided by his sons and grandchildren. Finally, he gave up his life as a householder and joined a monastic order. And in fact, at the age of eighty, he gained high levels of realization.

When my senior tutor, Ling Rinpoche, became the Abbot of Gyuto Monastery, his immediate predecessor was a very good scholar and a very good monk. Until that person was around twenty-five years old, he was one of the *dop dops*, or "stupid monks." They never are interested in learning or study, but just in playing and going here and there. This type of monk we call "dop dop." Sometimes, they are troublemakers also, not only in the monastery, but even in the town; sometimes they fight. They even use swords, and this is very stupid, very naughty.

So it was with this person. Until the age of twenty-five, he remained like that. Then, somehow he changed and put all his energy into study. Then, he became the top scholar. Such stories should give us more hope.

I think quite a number of the past great masters and teachers had many difficulties in their early life and family life. Then, at age thirty, forty, fifty, they started their serious practice and then became great masters. There are many stories. So even in old age, the physical situation declines, but still, comparatively, the human brain is still there.

Then, in addition, in Buddhist belief, there is the theory of rebirth. Given that there is a belief in rebirth in Buddhism, no time is too late. If you start even just one year before your death, the fruits of your efforts will not be wasted, because there is rebirth. They will be carried on and will be continued in the next life.

The great Sakya Pandita Kunga Gyaltsen said that knowledge is something that needs to be developed, that needs to be acquired, even if you are definitely going to die tomorrow. You can claim it in your next life, as if you asked someone to keep something for you.

However, for people who do not believe in rebirth, these arguments are quite silly.

Q: Your Holiness, please explain the concept of prayer in Buddhism. Who or what are the prayers directed to, since there is no Creator?

A: There are two types of prayer. I think prayer is, for the most part, simply reminders in your daily practice. So, the verses look like prayers, but are actually reminders of how to speak, how to deal with other problems, other people, things like that in daily life. For example, in my own daily practice, prayer, if I am leisurely, takes about four hours. Quite long. For the most part, I think my practice is reviewing: compassion, forgiveness, and, of course, shunyata. Then, in my case, the major portion is the visualization of deity, mandala, and attendant tantric practices including visualization of death and rebirth. In my daily practice, the deity mandala, deity yoga, and the visualization of death, rebirth, and intermediate state is done eight times. So, eight times death is eight times rebirth. I am supposed to be preparing for my death. When actual death comes, whether I will succeed or not, still, I don't know.

Then, some portion of prayer is appeal to Buddha. Although we do not consider Buddha as a Creator, at the same time we consider Buddha as a higher being who purified himself. So he has special energy, infinite energy or power. In certain ways, then, in this type of prayer, the appeal to Buddha can be seen as similar to the appeal to God as the Creator.

SECOND SESSION

Editor's Note: In the final teaching session, His Holiness began with the question and answer session in order to present a discourse on the twelve links of dependent origination at the end of the teaching.

QUESTIONS

Q: Is it necessary to seek an actual experience in order to fully understand it and have compassion toward it? For instance, many people in this room have generally lived lives free of suffering, such as poverty and political oppression. Does this mean we should be going beyond our television sets and newspapers and getting closer to really experiencing these things? Is this an effective way to counterbalance apathy?

A: At the initial stage, if you directly face suffering situations where you actually see suffering, then it will have greater impact on your developing compassion. However, there are different ways of reflecting on suffering. For instance, as I pointed out earlier, you could directly encounter a sight of someone suffering, which would give rise to your feeling of empathy and compassion, although you were not undergoing conscious or concrete sufferings as such. Then, toward those who are engaged in activities which are negative or harmful, one could also direct one's compassion, remembering that what they are doing is accumulating causes and conditions which will later lead them to undesirable consequences. The difference is only a matter of time. In one case, they are already at the resultant state, at the level of fruition; in the second case, they are not actually suffering, but they are at the causal stage during which they are already working toward that. So you can develop compassion toward that.

Even in the case of suffering, as I said earlier, there are different levels of suffering. For example, what we conventionally identify as pleasurable experiences are, in reality, sufferings of change. Underlying that is the basic unsatisfactory nature of existence in samsara. So once you begin to develop compassion based on such deeper levels of realization of suffering, then you don't need immediate experiences of suffering in order to motivate you to compassionate acts.

Q: You say that compassion consists of treating others with tolerance and kindness, and not doing harm to others. Should not compassion cause us to actively reach out to those in need, such as to alleviate the suffering of those who are ill, who live in extreme poverty, or who are victims of true injustice? Buddhism has sometimes been accused of neglecting the sufferings that exist in society. Please comment.

A: I think that to some extent this is true. As I mentioned earlier, Buddhist monks and nuns must take more active work in the society, like their Christian brothers and sisters do. For example, on my first visit to Thailand, I think during the late '60s, I particularly discussed this with the patriarch, and he explained that it is also true, according to the Vinaya texts, that monks and nuns must remain isolated from society. That is true, and my point is also true. So I explained, "Yes, that is true about the Vinaya texts. But at the same time, the very purpose of our practice is for the benefit of others. Therefore, at a practical level, if we can do more, it is very worthwhile."

One should not lose sight of the basic principle behind the monastic way of life, which is, so far as one's own interest is concerned, to have as little involvement as possible, as little business as possible. On the other hand, when it comes to the interest of serving others, then one should have as much involvement as possible.

Q: Do Buddhists attempt to "evangelize" or send missionaries to the world? There is so much spiritual hunger. If you don't, is there a reason?

A: I think during Ashoka's period, there were some Buddhist missions. But basically, in the Buddhist tradition there is no emphasis on evangelism, or sending missionaries to convert, or a movement for conversion, unless someone comes to seek the teaching. Then, of course, it is our duty or responsibility to explain. In the past, maybe it was different, but today the world has become much smaller, and the spirit of harmony is very essential. So, I believe, the Buddhist missionary is out of the question. But even about the missionary work of other religious traditions, I still have some reservations. If one side tries to propagate their religion, and another side also does a similar thing, then logically, there is the possibility of conflict. So I don't think this is something good.

My belief is, out of five billion human beings, I think there are only a few sincere, very genuine believers. Of course, I do not count those people who say "I am Christian" because their family background is Christian, because in daily life they may not consider the Christian faith very much. So excluding these people, of those who sincerely practice their religion, there are perhaps around one billion. That means that four billion, the majority of the people, are nonbelievers. So we must find a way to try to reach this majority of people, four billion people, to make them good human beings, or moral persons, without any religion. That is the point. Regarding compassion and related things, I consider them just good qualities of human beings, not necessarily religious subjects. So one can remain without any religious faith, but be a good, sensible human being and have a sense of responsibility or commitment for a better world, a happier world. In this regard, I think a proper way of education is very important. And media also is very important.

Q: I have been betrayed and treated unfairly by two people. This has created a great monetary loss for me and made it difficult to support my family. When I analyze this situation, I see that if I had been more aware, I could have recognized the betrayal earlier, cut off from these others, and saved myself from loss. So I am to blame. How can I stop hating myself for this loss? I know hating myself does no good, but I cannot stop.

A: It is not possible to stop hating oneself, if one is already in that situation, simply by adopting a particular thought once or twice. In fact, we have been discussing various techniques and methods over the last few days relevant to dealing with such situations. It is through a process of learning, training, and getting used to it that one will be able to deal with these difficulties.

Q: I have read in Buddhist books that it is inaccurate to believe we are learning any particular lessons in a given lifetime. Yet it feels that way, and seems consistent with karma. What is the correct or useful understanding?

A: I think there is some misunderstanding here, maybe related to the Buddhist idea of rebirth. According to Buddhism, there is definitely new knowledge which you gain through learning and practices, and you also gain many new experiences. For example, if we look at the Buddhist epistemological theory of mind and mental factors, according to one of the Abhidharma texts called *Compendium of Knowledge*, there are fifty-one types of mental factors. These are all different modalities of mind which we possess in our ordinary state as human beings. As we progress on the path, through our meditation and practice, there are many other types or modalities of mind which cannot be found within this list of fifty-one, but which we have to consciously and newly acquire as we go along on the path. For example, with regard to concentration or single-pointedness of mind, we find in Buddhist literature so many descriptions of various levels and stages of concentration and single-pointedness of mind, and all of these are to be developed newly, through practice and meditation.

Q: How does one meditate on emptiness?

A: I will deal with this in the presentation after the question/ answer session.

Q: Is there a way to train our minds so that we don't always feel tremendous sadness because of the overwhelming suffering in the world? In other words, how can we feel joyful in the face of so much suffering?

A: Bringing about transformation in one's outlook and way of thinking is not a simple matter. It requires application of so many different factors from different directions. For instance, according to Buddhist practices, we emphasize the unification of method (or skillful means) and wisdom. So you should not have the notion that there is just one secret, and if you can get that right, then everything will be okay. One should not have that kind of notion.

For example, in my own case, if I compare my usual mental attitude today, my mental attitude in this situation, to that of twenty or thirty years ago, there is a big difference. But these differences came about step by step. Although I started learning Buddhism at the age of five or six years, at that time I had no interest in it, although I was seen as the highest reincarnation. Then—I think around sixteen years old—I really began to feel serious and really tried to start serious practice. Then, in my twenties, even when I was in China and there were a lot of difficulties, still, whenever I had the occasion, I received teaching from my tutor. Then, unlike the previous time, I really made an effort from within. Then—I think around the age of thirty-four or thirty-five—I really just started to think about shunyata, emptiness. And as a result of intensive meditation based on serious effort, my understanding of the nature of cessation became something real. Then, I could feel some sense: "Yes, there is something, there is a possibility." That really gave me great inspiration. Still, at that time, bodhichitta was very difficult. I admire bodhichitta, that kind of mind is really marvelous. But the practice was still very far away in my thirties. Then, somehow in my forties, mainly as a result of studying and practicing Shantideva's text and some other books, eventually I came to have some experience of bodhichitta. Still, my mind is in bad shape. But somehow, now I have conviction that if I had enough time, appropriate time and an appropriate area, I could develop bodhichitta. This has been forty years.

So, when I meet people who claim to have attained high realizations within a short period of time, sometimes it makes me laugh, although I try to hide that feeling. But you see, deep down, mental development takes time. If someone says, "Oh, through hardship, through many years, then something will change," then I see something is working. If someone says, "Oh, within a short period, two years, something big changed," that is unrealistic.

Q: I have heard the mind described or defined as a container for thoughts. Is the object of meditation to remove the clutter of thoughts from the container of mind? Will doing this let the light shine?

A: In Buddhist terminology, we use the expression "purifying the stains of mind," rather than "emptying mind of its thought," because when we say "thoughts," we include both positive and negative thoughts. However, the aim of meditation is to arrive at what is known as the "state of nonconceptuality." And here, one must understand that when we use the term "nonconceptual," it can mean different things in different contexts. So the "nonconceptual state" means one thing in the context of the sutra explanation, and something different in the various classes of tantra. Even within Highest Yoga Tantra, it means something different in what are called the "Father Tantras" and the "Mother Tantras." We find the term "nonconceptual" quite frequently used in the context of Dzogchen teachings and Mahamudra teachings. And in these two cases, the association really is from the point of view of Highest Yoga Tantra understanding.

In a text on Mahamudra written by Dakpo Tashi Namgyal, a great scholar and practitioner, he claims that the Mahamudra path belongs neither to the sutra system nor to the tantra system. He describes it as a unique path, and he must have some grounds for making that claim. However, when you look at the statement, the notion of a path that belongs neither to sutra nor tantra is quite difficult to understand. In any case, that is not Buddhism. Buddha taught only the Sutrayana and the Tantrayana. But here is something which belongs to neither, which means that it is something different.

Anyway, in the Mahamudra practice, and in the Dzogchen practice, the main emphasis is on the combination of shunyata and clear light. Here again, when we use the term "clear light," it can mean two different things. In one way, it can refer to the object which is the emptiness, and "emptiness" can be understood in terms of clear light. In another way, it means the subjective experience of that emptiness. So "clear light" can have both objective and subjective connotations. The unification of both the subjective and objective aspects of clear light is what is emphasized in the Dzogchen and Mahamudra approaches. However, when using the words "object" and "subject" here, one should not have the uncomfortable feeling that, "Oh, still, there is duality," because so far as the phenomenological experience, or the state of the individual who is the meditator is concerned, from his or her perspective there is no duality. It is only from the perspective of a third person, or if you examine it in retrospect, that you would see that kind of a subject and object. But in the actual experience there is no duality between subject and object.

So when we talk about how to develop this state of nonconceptuality, there must be the potential or seed inherent within the individual practitioner to arrive at the state of nonconceptuality. However, we should not have the notion that, since the goal is to arrive at a nonconceptual state, nothing which involves conceptual thought processes can be of benefit to that goal. In fact, we find extensive discussion of this point in the second chapter of the *Exposition of Valid Means to Cognition* by Dharmakirti, where, with a lot of reasoning and argument, he demonstrates how conceptual thought processes, thinking, reflection, and meditations which involve intellectual thought processes ultimately culminate in an experience of nonconceptuality. This is something to bear in mind.

Also, we speak of two principal types of meditation: one is analytic, in which you employ your analytic faculty for investigation; the other is more absorptive, where single-pointedness is really the key. Since analysis involves using thought and thought processes, in Highest Yoga Tantra, when you cultivate special or penetrative insight, analysis is not used. Rather, it is done through a technique which emphasizes single-pointedness of mind. This is the type of method which you also find in Dzogchen and Mahamudra.

Q: Would you be kind enough to elaborate on the possibility of choice for doing good or bad deeds? Do your past deeds determine your actions and your view?

A: In fact, as you pointed out, much of our behavior, thought patterns, and views may be determined or governed by our past deeds. When talking about being influenced by past deeds, we are talking about the influence of conditioning. However, it is possible by exerting one's will and freedom of choice to distance oneself from the effects of those past deeds and try to habituate one's mind to ways with which you were not familiar in the past. You can consciously develop that familiarity and thus try to free yourself from the constraints of past deeds.

However, there are certain biological forces from which it may be more difficult to free oneself. In fact, according to Buddhism, the very physical body that we have is seen as an aggregate, a product of ignorance and delusions. It is seen not only as a basis of our current state of existence, which is characterized by limitations and suffering, but also as a kind of springboard for producing future experiences of suffering as well. There is something very biological within our body that obstructs us from trying to get out of that bondage, almost like something in-built, a sort of lethargy or something which makes it heavy. This also obstructs our clarity of mind. But it is possible to gain control over the very subtle levels of energy in the bodily elements through training the mind and through meditative experiences—especially in tantra, where, generally speaking, we can find within our bodily elements the gross levels, the subtle levels, and the very subtle levels. Then, in that way, one can outweigh the influences which are felt at the grosser levels of bodily elements. So there is that possibility too.

Q: In my understanding, enlightenment is, in a sense, freedom from the bondage of causes and conditions. How can one attain this state and still remain in this world where the nature of existence is relative and causal?

A: So far as the bounds of causes and conditions are concerned, they are universal, and reach even the stage of Buddhahood. For example, let us take the case of Buddha's omniscient mind, which is totally enlightened but interacts with objects. It is transient and momentarily changing, it is a process, so it is impermanent. You can see the principle of causality operating even there. However, sometimes the state of Buddhahood is defined as a state of immortality, the state of permanence. This should be understood in its proper context—it is described as a permanent state in terms of its continuum. Sometimes the state of Buddhahood is described as permanent because when we talk of the embodiments of the Buddha, there are both impermanent ones, which are subject to causes and conditions, and also permanent ones.

Now, when we speak of the embodiments of the Buddha, the *Buddhakayas*, we can find some which are momentarily changing and some which are not momentarily changing. So because there are two aspects when we talk of Buddhakaya or the "embodiments" of the Buddha, in its generality it is said to be unchanging and eternal.

Q: I am confused by your statement that causing injury is the perpetrator's essential nature and should not be held against him. Is not everyone's essential nature Buddha-nature?

A: I think there is a slight misunderstanding here. Shantideva used the argument in a hypothetical sense. There was a conditional clause there. Verse 39 reads:

> Even if it were the nature of the childish
> To cause harm to other beings,
> It would still be incorrect to be angry with them,
> For this would be like begrudging fire for having the nature
>   to burn.

There was that conditional "if."

However, when we use the term "essential nature," here again we have to understand that in different contexts it can mean very different things. When we say the essential nature of sentient beings' mind is pure, we are talking about Buddha-nature, which is at a very different level. Related to this point is the need to appreciate the subtle meanings of the various technical terms when we read texts dealing with the Buddhist philosophy of emptiness. For example, one of the key Sanskrit words critical to our understanding of the concept of emptiness is *svabhava,* which can be translated as "intrinsic being" or "self-nature," or simply as "essence." Thus it has varied connotations according to differing contexts. When you read these texts, you should be very careful to not be rigid about a particular understanding of the term and then try to apply that in all the contexts in which it is used. The same term may be used by one philosophical system, such as Madhyamika, in one way, and then in a different way by another school of thought. So it is important to have that flexibility and to appreciate the diversity of its meanings in different contexts.

Q: Can you explain something about Wednesday's Green Tara empowerment? What commitment is involved, etc.?

A: The ceremony which is being performed in relation to Green Tara tomorrow is that of a blessing, not a full empowerment. It also will be combined with a Long Life empowerment, the transmission of which comes from the Fifth Dalai Lama. So it is a practice which is unique to the lineage of the Dalai Lamas, and there is no specific commitment. So isn't that nice? You get the blessing, but there is no commitment!

However, if you take Bodhisattva vows in the morning, there will be commitment. These are principally the eighteen root vows and forty-six auxiliary vows or precepts of a Bodhisattva. So as I mentioned this morning, if this is your first exposure to Buddhist practices then maybe it is wiser not to take the vows.

Q: What advice would you offer to a Christian who studies Buddhism and who is considering taking the Bodhisattva vows this week?

A: It should be okay.

TWELVE LINKS OF DEPENDENT ORIGINATION

Up until now, we have been talking about the practice of patience and tolerance, which, as I pointed out earlier, is one of the six perfections, the main practices of Bodhisattvas. Again, as I pointed out, there are three principal types of patience or tolerance: acceptance of harm and injuries inflicted by others; voluntarily taking upon oneself the pain, sufferings, and hardships that are involved in the practice; and developing and enhancing one's capacity for patience and tolerance by developing one's appreciation of the nature of reality, such as the complexity of situations. This could also include insight into the ultimate nature of reality, such as emptiness and so on.

One thing which I haven't pointed out is that a genuine or ideal practice of each of the perfections must be complete; it must contain within itself all of the aspects of the other five perfections. For instance, in the case of the practice of patience, while remaining in the state of patience and tolerance, encouraging others also to do so is the practice of giving or generosity. The second is basing your practice of patience and tolerance on honesty and sincerity, which are aspects of ethical discipline involved in the practice of patience. The third, of course, is patience itself. The fourth, which is joyous effort, refers to all the efforts which are involved in maintaining patience and tolerance. The fifth is that when you engage in such a practice, you maintain a single-pointedness of mind and the ability to focus on whatever you are doing and remain single-pointed. Mindfulness can also be included here, which is the aspect of concentration and single-pointedness in one's practice of patience. The wisdom practice is your ability to judge what is appropriate and what is inappropriate as well as what is required in a given situation. These are all faculties of wisdom and intelligence that are a concomitant part of your practice of patience. This could also include the wisdom of realizing the empty nature of phenomena, if you have it. This is the same in the case of the practices of all the other perfections, such as generosity: within the practice of generosity, all of the other perfections must be complete. And the same is true for ethical discipline, and so on.

When we talk of the six perfections—generosity, ethical discipline, patience, perseverance, concentration, and wisdom—they also can be found in other, non-Bodhisattva practitioners who are working more toward their own individual liberation. What makes the practice of these six factors perfected is the motivation involved. In order for one's practice of patience to be a practice of the perfection of patience, you need the motivation which is bodhichitta. If your practice of patience and generosity and so on is motivated by bodhichitta, the aspiration to attain enlightenment for the benefit of all, then your practice becomes truly a practice of perfection.

All of these practices of the six perfections belong either to practices associated with the accumulation of merit or practices principally associated with the accumulation of wisdom. The reason there is this division into two principal categories on the path, the method aspect and the wisdom aspect, is because the resultant state of Buddhahood is characterized in terms of two kayas of the Buddha, or the two embodiments. One is the dharmakaya state, which can be seen as the state of ultimate realization of the Buddha's being, or self-realization. The other embodiment is called *rupakaya*, which is the form body. These two kayas or embodiments have different functions: the dharmakaya state is like the self-realization of one's own perfected state; the rupakaya, the form body, is specifically assumed in order to be of service, in order to make the Buddha accessible to other sentient beings. It is a kind of medium through which the dharmakaya can interact with and benefit other sentient beings. So what you have here is a general framework of the Mahayana path according to the sutra system, in which your whole motivation to embark on the spiritual path to perfection is that of bodhichitta, the aspiration to attain full enlightenment for the sake of all. Then, motivated by that intention, you engage in a path that is characterized by the practice of six perfections, which constitute the unification of method and wisdom. And through the stages of the ten Bodhisattva levels, you arrive at the resultant state of fruition, where there is an embodiment of dharmakaya and rupakaya. That is the general approach you find in the sutra system according to the Mahayana path.

Now what is unique and what makes the Buddhist tantric approach different from the Mahayana sutra approach is that, according to tantra, the unification of method and wisdom is understood at a deeper, more profound level. This is because in the sutra system the unification of method and wisdom is understood in terms of two distinct entities, two totally different cognitive events. So although method and wisdom complement each other, the unification is understood in terms of complementarity, one complementing the other, one supporting and reinforcing the other. However, in tantra, the unification is taken to a much deeper level, where the understanding is that within one event of consciousness or mental state, both the method and the wisdom aspects are complete. It is not as if there are two distinct states of mind, one complementing the other, but rather there is a kind of assimilation within a single cognitive event of both method and wisdom. That is what forms the basis in all the stages of tantra.

Within the tantra, there are different systems or divisions. Sometimes the tantric path is divided into six classes; generally, it is divided into four. The differentiating characteristic between the first three classes of tantra and Highest Yoga Tantra is that in Highest Yoga Tantra there is an extensive presentation and emphasis on the practice of clear light, which is absent in the three lower classes of tantra.

In order to understand the idea of clear light properly, one has to understand the possibility of being able to perceive consciousness, and energies that go along with the consciousness, at many different levels of subtlety. Because of this, in Highest Yoga Tantra literature we find a lot of discussion of the chakras, the energy channels, the energies that flow within them, and the essential drops that are located at principal sites within the body. This is because they are all inextricably linked with the idea of differentiating various levels of consciousness and energy. So it is because of these principles that you find in the Highest Yoga Tantra approach imageries and iconography which depict either very wrathful or erotic forms. Many of these Highest Yoga Tantra practices that are related with energy channels, chakras, subtle energies, and so on, take into account certain basic constituents that form our bodily existence, such as the six elements. Due to the flow of these elements and energies within our body, and due to their movements and energy levels, these affect the states of our mind, the levels of our consciousness. For example, we find that there are certain situations or occasions in our life where we can have glimpses of what could be called the experience of the subtle mind. This is described by Buddha-shrijnana in one of his texts, in which he says that in our ordinary state we have certain occasions when we naturally get a glimpse of the experience of the subtle mind, such as in deep sleep, sexual climax, when we faint, and at the time of death. During these stages, we naturally experience a form of subtle consciousness. So out of these four naturally occurring situations, if the meditator applies certain meditative techniques, it is possible for him or her to create opportunities for grasping the moment and consciously generating the experience of subtle clear light. This is especially so during the time of death, and then, in order, during the times of deep sleep and sexual climax.

So it is in the light of these factors that one has to understand the idea of the *yab-yum* principle, the male-and-female union. If our understanding is correct, we find that the kind of sexual act that the male-female deities are engaged in is very different from what we would understand by a sexual act in the ordinary sense. What is required here is the capability on the part of the participants in this kind of yab-yum act to hold the energy and protect it from emission. In fact, when a tantric practitioner fails in holding the energy and spills it, this is considered a great fault. This is very much emphasized and is considered a very grave mistake on the part of the practitioner, especially in Kalachakra Tantra.

So what we understand here is that the greater or more profound the unification of method and wisdom is, the more effective and powerful one's path is toward enlightenment. However, a successful practice of all of these principles is foundationally grounded in the generation and realization of bodhichitta. Without that prerequisite, there is no way one can successfully engage in these practices.

In order to successfully generate bodhichitta, one needs a sense of commitment and responsibility, taking upon oneself the responsibility to help others become free from suffering. That is a precondition for generating bodhichitta. That, in turn, requires the condition of having developed universal compassion.

We find in the tradition two principal techniques or methods for cultivating such universal compassion: the "seven-point cause and effect" method, and the "exchange and equality of oneself with others." These are the two principal techniques or methods for cultivating compassion. Exchanging oneself for and equalizing oneself with others is the technique which you find in the eighth chapter of Shantideva's *Guide to the Bodhisattva's Way of Life*.

So these are all various aspects of the Mahayana path toward the attainment of full enlightenment. However, in order to generate genuine compassion, which is the feeling that the sight of other sentient beings' suffering is unbearable, what is required on the part of the individual first of all is to be able to appreciate the seriousness, or the intensity, of suffering. So here a realization of the nature of suffering is necessary.

The type of compassion that we normally have is such that when we come across the sight of someone who is really in pain, we feel spontaneous empathy. We think, "Oh, how bad, how pitiful." However, when you come across someone who is successful in worldly terms, instead of feeling sorry and compassionate, you feel envious and jealous. So that is really a childish compassion. The reason we have this kind of feeling is that we haven't really understood the true meaning of suffering. So in order to develop that genuine appreciation of suffering, the meaning of suffering, we have to train ourselves in the foundational paths.

It is not sufficient to simply develop the realization of the suffering nature and recognize the true meaning of suffering. It is also important to develop an appreciation of the possibility of the alternative, that is, liberation from suffering. Here, an understanding of the principles of the Four Noble Truths becomes relevant. This is a path which is common to both Mahayana Buddhist and non-Mahayana Buddhist approaches.

When we speak of the Four Noble Truths, we find that there are two sets of cause and effect. One set relates to our experience and existence in samsara, suffering being the result and the origin of suffering being the cause. So one set of causes and effects deals with the manner in which we remain in the cycle of existence. Another set deals with the process that allows us to get out of that bondage and attain freedom from suffering. These two are cessation as the result, and the path leading to cessation as the cause. When we understand these two sets of causes and effects in a more extensive way, then we focus on the principles of the twelve links of dependent origination. In other words, the twelve links of dependent origination is an elaboration on the themes summarized in the Four Noble Truths.

In the twelve links of dependent origination, there is both a reverse order and the order in its proper sequence. If one reflects on its proper sequence of order, then one sees that ignorance is the first. Ignorance leads to volitional acts; this leads to implanting imprints on consciousness; which leads to name and form; culminating in aging and death. By reflecting on this chain, we understand the mechanism by which we take rebirth in the cycle of existence and then go through the vicious cycle of life and death.

When we reverse the order and reflect upon the cessation of each of the twelve links, then we will see that the cessation of aging and death depends upon the cessation of becoming; the cessation of that depends on the cessation of grasping or clinging, and so on. So in its reverse order, we understand the process by which one can get out of this bondage and obtain freedom and liberation from samsara.

All the practices which are based on appreciation of the sequential and reverse order of the twelve links of dependent origination are found in what are known as "the practices of the thirty-seven aspects of the path to enlightenment." And this begins with the practice of the four mindfulnesses and so on. So the thirty-seven aspects of the path to enlightenment are, in other words, practices associated with the twelve links of dependent origination.

The first of the thirty-seven aspects of the path to enlightenment is mindfulness of the body. Next is mindfulness of our feeling and emotions. Then, mindfulness of mind or consciousness. Then, mindfulness of phenomena.

When one meditates on mindfulness of the body, reflecting upon the manner in which the body comes into being, and examining the causal conditions, then one will also see the impurities of the body. Then, from that perspective, one will find that even those who seem successful in worldly terms are not really objects worthy of envy; they are still within the bondage of suffering and dissatisfaction. In fact, if we think about this more seriously, we find that the greater the success that one enjoys in worldly terms, the more complex the psychological make-up seems to be, because there is a much more complex nexus of hopes and fears and apprehensions and inhibitions.

What Āryadeva says in his *Four Hundred Verses* seems to be very true. He states that those who are successful or fortunate in worldly terms are plagued by mental and emotional pains, and those who are poor are plagued by physical suffering and pains. This seems to be very true.

What makes all sentient beings live a life characterized by suffering and pain is that ultimately they are all under the power or influence of ignorance. One should try to develop a sense of urgency, as if one were an AIDS patient. Once one has that illness, there is a sense of urgency because one's days are numbered. Similarly, one should think, "As long as I am under the influence and power of ignorance and misknowledge, then sooner or later something is bound to turn up. So I must work now." One must develop that sense of urgency.

As long as one remains under the influence and power of the three poisons of the mind, there is no room for real happiness. So in a way, we are like slaves of the three poisons of mind. And while there exists a possibility or a method of freeing ourselves from bondage, then not making the effort to obtain such freedom seems to be quite wretched and foolish.

So when one meditates and thinks along these lines, when one says the words, "the three realms of existence in samsara," then from somewhere in the depths of one's heart comes a sense of "Oh, I must get out of it. I must attain freedom from this." What we generate from our heart is the desire to free ourselves from the bondage of these three poisons of mind.

However, in order to successfully attain that liberation, it requires a long period of meditation and practice—in some cases, even several lifetimes. What becomes urgent in that case is to make sure that we obtain a favorable form of existence in the future so we will have the opportunity to carry on and pursue this goal from where we left off.

So although our ultimate goal is liberation and we set that as our objective, in order to arrive there the first step is to ensure that we have a favorable rebirth. And in order to do that, what is required is principally living an ethically disciplined way of life in which one refrains from the ten negative actions or ten nonvirtues. These ten nonvirtues include three actions of body (killing, stealing, and sexual misconduct); four of speech (lying, divisive speech, harsh speech, and meaningless gossip); and three of mind (covetousness, harmful intent, and distorted views). In order to generate a genuine enthusiasm to live a way of life within the kind of ethical discipline characterized by refraining from the ten nonvirtues, it is important to develop a good understanding of the mechanisms of karma, cause and effect.

Now, when it comes to trying to understand the mechanisms behind the concept of karma, and how actions and effects relate to each other, and how one leads to the other at a very subtle level, these remain beyond the scope of our ordinary understanding. At the initial stage, the most subtle aspects of the karmic theory remain beyond our comprehension. Therefore, a degree of faith, or reliance on the Buddha's word regarding the doctrine of karma, seems to be necessary. Because of this, observing the law of karma is very closely associated with taking refuge. In fact, living a disciplined way of life within the law of karma is seen as the precept of taking refuge.

In order to engage in such practices as taking refuge, living a way of life which accords with the law of karma, and living in an ethically disciplined way characterized by observance of the ten virtues, and so on, we require a tremendous sense of confidence that we can do it. To generate that, and also a kind of enthusiasm, we find in the Buddha's texts a discussion of the preciousness of the human body and human existence. At that stage, we never talk about how impure the body and bodily substances are, or how imperfect they are. In fact, we are talking about how good it is, how meaningful, how purposeful, how much potential lies within our body, what good purpose it can be used for, and so on. This is to instill a sense of confidence and courage. Therefore, at that stage, one should not focus on the negative aspects of the body, particularly if one has the problem of low self-esteem or self-hatred. If one talks about imperfections of the body, impurities, and so on to such a person, it might aggravate the problem and make it even worse. At that stage, we are talking mainly about the characteristics, benefits, and advantages of the human form, in order to generate not only a sense of urgency to appreciate the potentials of our body, but also a sense of commitment to use it in a positive way.

Then, the practitioner is reminded of impermanence and death. When we talk about impermanence here, we are using very conventional terms: one day, we will no longer be here. This awareness of impermanence is encouraged, so that when it is coupled with an appreciation of the enormous potential of human existence, it will give a sense of urgency: "I must utilize every precious moment of my life." That kind of enthusiasm, eagerness, and confidence must be developed.

To reach that point, it is important to study first. But as Dromtonpa said, when he is studying and learning, he does not forget the practices of contemplation and meditation. Similarly, when he is contemplating a given topic, he hasn't forgotten the importance of study and meditation. And when he is meditating, he doesn't forget the importance of learning and contemplation. In other words, he always combines the three. That is a concerted, coordinated, and combined approach. This is very important so that there won't be any imbalances between intellectual learning and practical implementation. Otherwise, there is a danger of too much intellectualization, which will kill the practice, or too much emphasis on practical implementation without study, which will kill the understanding. There has to be a balance.

The overview that I have given, the procedure of the path as given in reverse order, starting from the top down, is found in Āryadeva's *Four Hundred Verses*, where he sums up the entire Buddhist path. He states that at the initial stage, what is important is to reverse one's negative and destructive actions of body, speech, and mind. So that is the importance of living an ethically disciplined way of life. At the second stage, the importance should be shifted to overcoming delusory states and their underlying ignorance, which apprehends things and events as if they were inherently existent and possessed intrinsic reality and identity. Then, at the third stage, all forms of imprints, tendencies, and dispositions which are implanted on one's psyche by delusory states are to be removed. So there are three distinct stages in one's evolutionary process toward full enlightenment.

Meditation

Let us pause a moment for silent meditation. During the past sessions, as we have been having discussions, you might have had some experience of joy or happiness, some pleasant experience. Some of you might have felt tired, exhausted. So now, let us try to focus on and examine what that "I" or "self" is that has experienced this joy. Let us focus our attention on this and search for it.

What is definite is that it does not exist independently of our body and mind. And out of the two, the body and mind, it is clear that the body cannot be seen as this "self." Feelings are also not the self because in our ordinary notion of self, we say "I feel," as if there is an agent, as if there is a "feeler" and a feeling. So feeling cannot be the person. Nor can you identify perception as the self, because again we say, "I perceive," and it seems that there is an act of perception and someone who perceives. So perception cannot be identified with the "self" or the person.

Now, if you were given the choice to exchange your mind for a mind that was more perfect and clear and aware, most of us seem to be willing to do that. Similarly, we also feel this way toward our body; if there were a possibility of exchanging it for something much more desirable or attractive. . . . Again, although so far medical technology hasn't allowed us to be able to transplant brains, there is a kind of willingness; if it were possible, we would like to exchange it.

What this shows is that the way we naturally perceive ourselves, the way the sense of "self" arises, is that there is something like the agent, or the subject, which experiences and perceives. Then, the aggregates are something that, in some sense, are owned by the "self," or something which are part of the "self."

Similarly, when you feel intense anger or hatred, there is that strong sense of "I": "I am angry." Then, when your hatred and anger are directed toward, let us say, your enemy, you feel him or her with a kind of grasping, an idea of some kind of solid, concrete person who is one hundred percent negative, or one hundred percent positive, depending on how you feel. So if the person, our object of hatred and anger, existed in the way we perceive, then whatever quality we project onto the person should be part of that reality. That means that the object of our anger and hatred will remain one hundred percent negative, and there is no room for change. But this is not the case.

So to our naive, natural mind, everything appears to us as if it has an independent, solid, objective entity, an objective status— as if it is existing in its own right, objectively and independently. However, if things and events existed in the way we perceive them, then the more we search for them, the clearer they should become. What is very clear is that when we begin to search, they sort of disintegrate and disappear, and they are unfindable.

Even in modern scientific terms, physicists, in their pursuit of understanding the nature of physical reality, have reached a stage where they have lost the concept of solid matter; they can't come up with the real identity of matter. So they are beginning to see things in more holistic terms, in terms of interrelationships rather than discreet, independent, concrete objects.

If things and events existed as we perceive them, objectively enjoying some sort of independent status as discrete, concrete identities, then when we look for them, when we look for the true referents behind the terms, they should become clearer and clearer. That doesn't seem to be the case. The moment we begin to look for them, the concept seems to disintegrate and disappear. What that indicates is not that things and events do not exist. Because the fact that they exist is very real, our experience tells us that events make differences: because of different events, we either suffer pain or enjoy pleasure and joy. The reality of phenomena is such that our experience affirms their reality. So the conclusion that we can draw from this is that there is a disparity between the way we perceive things and the way things and events actually exist. There is a disparity between our perception and the reality, in other words, between appearance and reality. So once we have gained some inkling of understanding of this disparity, then keeping that in mind, we should simply judge how we normally relate to the world and others—how we perceive people, the environment around us, and ourselves. In this analysis, we see that we tend to relate to the world, ourselves, and others in a manner that indicates that we believe that there is something independent and objective. Then we realize that this is not the way things exist. Things do not exist in the way they appear to us. Then, simply place your focus on your conclusion that things do not exist inherently or intrinsically and do not enjoy the independent status that we perceive in them.

Since they exist, what is the manner in which they exist? What is the status of their existence? We are forced to conclude that we can understand their existence and identity only in terms of interrelationships: something that is derived through interaction with others and in dependence upon other factors and labels and designations that we impose on reality. Then simply place your mind on that conclusion that things do not exist independently, inherently, and do not enjoy that intrinsic reality or intrinsic identity. That is what is meant by meditating on emptiness.

So when we meditate on emptiness, we are not thinking, "Oh, this is emptiness"; we are not thinking, "Oh, things do not exist in this way, but may exist in another way." There should not be any attempt at affirming something. What there should be is a simple placement of the mind on this conclusion that things and events are lacking independent or intrinsic reality, which is not the same as placing the mind on total vacuity or mere absence. Rather, one places the mind on the absence of independent existence and intrinsic reality.

GLOSSARY

Note: Explanations in this glossary were drawn from those appearing in *A Handbook of Tibetan Culture,* compiled by the Orient Foundation and edited by Graham Coleman (Boston: Shambhala, 1994). For further elaboration of technical terms, please refer to that work.

Abhidharma (Skt.) One of the three divisions of the Buddhist canon (the Tripitaka, or "Three Baskets"), which contains scriptures dealing with such subjects as phenomenology, psychology, knowledge, and cosmology.

aggregates (Skt. *skandha*) The five principal faculties which constitute a sentient being, namely those of form, feeling, perception/discrimination, conditioning/motivational factors, and consciousness.

Arhat (Skt.) A being who has attained liberation from the cycle of existence by eliminating the karmic tendencies and afflictive emotions which give rise to compulsive existence in a cycle of birth, death, and rebirth. The goal to which practitioners of the Hinayana aspire.

bindus (Skt.) Literally "drops," referring to the pure essence of the white/male and red/female generative or seminal fluids of the body which, along with the energy channels and winds that flow through them, form an important aspect of human physiology according to Buddhist medical theory and tantra.

bodhichitta (Skt.) The altruistic aspiration to attain full enlightenment in order to benefit all beings.

bodhisattva (Skt.) A spiritual trainee who has generated the altruistic mind of bodhichitta and is on the path to full enlightenment. Dedicated fully to bringing about the welfare of all sentient beings, bodhisattvas vow to remain within the cycle of existence to help beings instead of seeking liberation for themselves alone.

cessation *See* Four Noble Truths.

chakra (Skt.) Literally "wheel" or "circle." In the context of tantra, it refers to the energy centers within the human body. The principal chakras are said to be located at the crown, throat, heart, navel, and sexual organ.

Chandrakirti The sixth-century Indian Buddhist scholar who clarified Nagarjuna's presentation of Middle Way philosophy.

Chittamatra (Skt.) One of the four major Buddhist philosophical schools of ancient India. Founded in the fourth century by the Indian scholar and saint Asanga, its main tenet is that all phenomena are either actual mental events or extensions of the mind. Often translated as the "Mind-Only school."

delusions (Skt. *klesa*, Tib. *nyon mongs*) Psychological afflictions that disturb the mind and obstruct the expression of its essentially pure nature. The three primary afflictions or "three poisons" are greed/attachment, hatred/aversion, and delusion, or fundamental ignorance which misperceives the nature of reality.

Dharma (Skt.) A term with a wide range of uses. In doctrinal contexts it refers to the realizations of the Buddhas, both the state of cessation and the paths leading to it, and the transmission of authoritative texts and their oral commentarial lineages which expound the path to Buddhahood.

dharmakaya (Skt.) *See* three kayas.

Dharmakirti The sixth–seventh-century Indian philosopher and logician whose works form the basis for the study of logic and epistemology in the Tibetan Buddhist tradition.

Dzogchen (Tib.) Literally "Great Perfection" or "Great Completion." The highest system of practice within the Nyingma tradition of Tibetan Buddhism.

emptiness *See* shunyata.

Father Tantras A classification within Highest Yoga Tantra which includes those tantras that place greater emphasis on the yogas associated with skillful means and the attainment of the illusory body.

Four Noble Truths The truth of suffering, the truth of the origins of suffering, the truth of the cessation of suffering, and the truth of the path leading to the cessation of suffering. The teaching on the Four Noble Truths was the basis of the first public discourse of Buddha Shakyamuni after his enlightenment.

Highest Yoga Tantra (Skt. *anuttarayogatantra*) The highest of the four classes of tantra, which are differentiated by means of the different emphases each places on external practices, visualization, internal yoga practices, and techniques for manifesting the three kayas.

Hinayana Literally the "Lesser" or "Smaller" vehicle, so-called on the basis of the primary motivation of the practitioner, which is for individual liberation from cyclic existence as opposed to the "Greater Vehicle" motivation of liberating all sentient beings. *See* Mahayana.

Jataka **Tales** Past-life stories of the Buddha which make up one of the twelve traditional divisions of the Buddha's discourses. They illustrate how, in previous lives, the Buddha dedicated himself to the bodhisattva's way of life.

Kadampa (Tib.) Followers of the Kadam school of Tibetan Buddhism founded by the eleventh-century Indian scholar and saint Atisha and his Tibetan disciple Dromtonpa. This school is particularly known for its emphasis on the practical application of the ideals of the bodhisattva and was responsible for the development of a collection of writings and practices known as "lojong"—"mind training" or "thought transformation."

karma (Skt.) Literally "actions." Actual physical, verbal, and mental actions and the psychological imprints and tendencies created within the mind by such actions, which remain within the mental continuum through successive rebirths. Such a karmic potential is later activated when it meets appropriate circumstances and conditions. The doctrine of karma has two main features: (1) one never experiences the consequences of an action not committed; and (2) the potential of an action once committed is never lost unless obviated by specific remedies.

Madhyamika (Skt.) The most influential of the four major philosophical schools of Indian Buddhism. Its name literally means the "Middle Way," between the extremes of eternalism and nihilism. Prasangika Madhyamika is one of the two main sub-schools of Madhyamika.

Mahamudra (Skt.) Literally "Great Seal," it is defined differently according to sutra or tantra explanations. As a meditative approach it applies both shamatha and vipashyana while focusing on the nature of the meditator's own mind. Mahamudra meditation is found within both the Kagyu and Gelug schools of Tibetan Buddhism.

Mahayana (Skt.) One of the two main systems or vehicles of Buddhism, the other being known as *Hinayana*. In terms of motivation it emphasizes altruism and has as its goal the liberation of all beings. It is therefore called the "Great Vehicle."

Maitreya One of the eight bodhisattva disciples of Buddha Shakyamuni, to whom are attributed five great works which are foundational for the Chittamatra school of Indian philosophy.

Mother Tantras A classification within Highest Yoga Tantra which includes those tantras that place greater emphasis on the yogas associated with the attainment of the mind of clear light.

Nagarjuna The second-century founder of the Madhyamika school of Buddhist thought.

nirvana (Skt.) Literally the "state beyond sorrow." Refers to the permanent cessation of all suffering and the dissonant emotions which cause and perpetuate suffering.

Nyingma (Tib.) The oldest school of Tibetan Buddhism, based on the teaching traditions and texts introduced to Tibet during the eighth and ninth centuries.

Prasangika Madhyamika *See* Madhyamika.

pratyekabuddha (Skt.) Sometimes translated into English as "solitary realizer," indicates one who attains the state of liberation without reliance on verbal instruction. *See also* shravaka.

Rendawa (Tib. Red mda' ba) A great fifteenth-century teacher of the Sakya school of Tibetan Buddhism. He was one of the main teachers of Tsongkhapa, the founder of the Gelug school.

rupakaya (Skt.) "Form body" in Mahayana Buddhism, used to refer to both the sambhogakaya (enjoyment body) and the nirmanakaya (emanation body). *See also* three kayas.

Sakya Pandita Kunga Gyaltsen (1182–1251) One of the five great founders of the Sakya school of Tibetan Buddhism.

samsara (Skt.) "Cyclic existence," a state of existence conditioned by karmic tendencies and imprints from past actions—recurring habitual patterns—which is characterized by a cycle of life and death and by suffering.

sangha (Skt.) The spiritual community of ordained practitioners, both monks and nuns. When viewed as an object of refuge in the context of the three precious jewels, it is a sublime, highly realized assembly of those who have gained direct insight into the true nature of reality, emptiness, and is represented by the monastic community.

shamatha (Skt.) A meditative state characterized by the stabilization of attention on an internal object of observation. In addition, shamatha is characterized by suppleness of mind and body, and the calming of external distractions to the mind. Also called "calm abiding."

shravaka (Skt.) "Hearer," referring in the sutra-based texts of Buddhist literature to one of the three types of spiritual trainee—the others being *pratyekabuddha* and *bodhisattva*. Inclined to seek merely their own liberation from cyclic existence, shravakas depend heavily on verbal instruction and aim in their practice to eliminate mistaken belief in a personal identity.

shunyata (Skt.) Translated into English as "emptiness," referring to the ultimate nature of reality, which is the total absence of inherent existence and self-identity with respect to all phenomena. Its precise meaning varies according to different schools of philosophic tenets.

six perfections The six practices which form the basis of the bodhisattva's way of life: (1) generosity; (2) ethical discipline; (3) patience; (4) perseverance or joyous effort; (5) meditative concentration; and (6) discriminative awareness or wisdom.

sutra (Skt.) The original discourses taught publicly by Buddha Shakyamuni.

Sutrayana (Skt.) In Mahayana Buddhism, the entire path to enlightenment is presented within the framework of two main systems or vehicles, the Sutrayana and the Tantrayana. The Sutrayana includes those systems and practices based on the sutras.

tantra (Skt.) Literally "continuum." Tantra has two basic meanings in Buddhism—it refers to the systems of practice and to the literature which expounds those practices. The tantras present sophisticated techniques which enable the practitioner to transform dissonant emotions into blissful states of realization. These teachings are said to have been given by Buddha Shakyamuni while appearing in the form of esoteric meditational deities.

Tantrayana (Skt.) A division of Mahayana Buddhism, based upon the tantric texts. Also referred to as Vajrayana and Mantrayana.

Tathagata (Skt.) A synonym for Buddha, used frequently in the sutras. "Tatha" literally means "thus," and "gata," "gone" or "departed." The word is interpreted in different ways, corresponding to the different classes of Mahayana sutras and tantras.

Theravada (Skt.) The "way expounded by the elders," the surviving school of ancient Indian Buddhism, maintained principally in Thailand, Burma, Cambodia, and Sri Lanka. Its canon is fully extant in the Pali language.

three jewels The Buddha, or the expression of the ultimate nature; Dharma, the true path and the consequent states of freedom it leads to; and the Sangha, the ideal spiritual community. These three are regarded as the perfect objects in which refuge may be sought from the unsatisfactory nature of life in cyclic existence.

three kayas The "three bodies" of a buddha, used in this context to refer not only to the physical body of a buddha, but also to the differing "dimensions" in which the embodiment of fully enlightened attributes occurs. These three are the dharmakaya (truth body); sambhogakaya (enjoyment body); and nirmanakaya (emanation body).

three poisons *See* delusions.

tong-len (Tib. *gtong len*) "Giving and taking." A Mahayana practice, in which one visualizes giving one's happiness to others and taking upon oneself the suffering, unhappiness, and misfortunes of others. This practice aims to develop loving-kindness and compassion.

Two Truths The conventional or relative truth (appearances) and the ultimate truth (emptiness). All Buddhist philosophical schools formulate their metaphysics within the framework of the two truths, yet their definitions of these differ according to their differing epistemological interpretations.

Vaibhashika school One of the four major Buddhist philosophical schools of ancient India.

Vinaya (Skt.) Literally, "discipline," referring in general to the codes of ethical conduct that regulate the life of ordained monks and nuns. Also refers to the division of the Buddhist canon containing Buddha's discourses on discipline.

Vipashyana (Skt.) "Penetrative insight," an analytical meditative state which penetrates the nature, characteristics or function of its chosen object of meditation and is generated on the basis of shamatha.

Yogachara (Skt.) In this context, a synonym for *Chittamatra.*

Works Cited

Sutras

"The Pratimoksha Sutra" *Prātimokṣa-sūtra*
"The Rice Sapling Sutra" *Śālistamba-sūtra*

Treatises by Indian Commentators

Āryadeva
    "Four Hundred Verses" *Catuḥśataka*
Asaṅga
    "Compendium of Knowledge" *Abhidharmasamuccaya*
Chandrakirti
    "Entry into the Middle Way" *Madhyamakāvatāra*
Dharmakirti
    "Exposition of Valid Means to Cognition" *Pramāṇavārttika*
Guṇaprabhā
    "Vinaya Sutra" *Vinayasūtra*
Maitreya
    "Ornament of Clear Realizations" *Abhisamayālaṃkāra*
    "Ornament of Scriptures" *Mahāyānāsūtralaṃkāra*
    "Sublime Continuum" *Uttaratantra*
Shantideva
    "Guide to the Bodhisattva's Way of Life" *Bodhisattvacaryāvatāra*
    "Compendium of Deeds" *Śikṣāmuccaya*

RECOMMENDED READING

Dalai Lama. *The Complete Foundation*. Boulder: Shambhala Publications, 2018.

———. *For the Benefit of All Beings*. Boulder: Shambhala Publications, 2009.

———. *Kindness, Clarity, and Insight*. Boulder: Snow Lion Publications, 2013.

———. *The World of Tibetan Buddhism*. Boston: Wisdom Publications, 1995.

Hopkins, Jeffrey. *Emptiness Yoga*. Ithaca, NY: Snow Lion Publications, 1987.

Garfield, Jay. *The Fundamental Wisdom of the Middle Way*. New York: Oxford University Press, 1995.

Khyentse, Dilgo. *Enlightened Courage*. Ithaca, NY: Snow Lion Publications, 1993.

Piburn, Sidney, ed. *The Dalai Lama: A Policy of Kindness*. Ithaca, NY: Snow Lion Publications, 1990.

Powers, John. *Introduction to Tibetan Buddhism*. Ithaca, NY: Snow Lion Publications, 1995.

Rinchen, Geshe Sonam. *The Thirty-Seven Practices of Bodhisattvas*. Translated & edited by Ruth Sonam. Ithaca, NY: Snow Lion Publications, 1997.

Shantideva. *A Guide to the Bodhisattva's Way of Life*. Translated by Stephen Batchelor. Dharamsala, India: Library of Tibetan Works and Archives, 1979.

Books by the Dalai Lama

Index